A Little Good

A Little Good

The Sisters of St. Mary in Texas

SISTER ST. JOHN BEGNAUD, SSMN

Foreword by
MONSIGNOR JOSEPH SCHUMACHER

WIPF & STOCK · Eugene, Oregon

A LITTLE GOOD
The Sisters of St. Mary in Texas

Copyright © 2011 Sister St. John Begnaud, SSMN. All rights reserved. Except for brief quotations in critical publications or reviews, no part of this book may be reproduced in any manner without prior written permission from the publisher. Write: Permissions, Wipf and Stock Publishers, 199 W. 8th Ave., Suite 3, Eugene, OR 97401.

Wipf & Stock
An Imprint of Wipf and Stock Publishers
199 W. 8th Ave., Suite 3
Eugene, OR 97401

www.wipfandstock.com

ISBN 13: 978-1-61097-850-7

Manufactured in the U.S.A.

The cover photograph is of Sister Mary Angela Healy, the first Superior in Waco and the sister of Mrs. Margaret Mary Healy Murphy, the wife of Mr. John Murphy, who was very instrumental in getting the sisters to Texas. The original photograph was taken in about 1900 and is kept in the archives of Our Lady of Victory Center, Fort Worth.

"... to those sisters who so cheerfully made every sacrifice,

hoping to do

A Little Good

in Texas"

Contents

Foreword by Monsignor Joseph Schumacher ix
Acknowledgments xi

Introduction 1
1 Beginnings 5
2 Decisions 18
3 From Ireland to Texas 38
4 Unlikely Spread 62
5 "Hell's Half Acre" 90
6 Beyond the Cluster 102
7 And Farther North 117
8 A New Turn 126
9 A Home of Our Own 132
10 Personal Stories 153
   Time Chart 167

   Works Consulted 171

Foreword

A Little *Good* is the story of a small group of women whose dedication to education, and especially to evangelization, simply ignored insurmountable obstacles. Founded in Belgium when religious communities were forbidden, arriving in New York during the American Civil War, and establishing Catholic schools in areas of Texas unfriendly to Catholic presence, they changed the way the Church was perceived in North Texas.

Always struggling with debt, the sisters seemed to accept without question the fact that they were to build, as well as teach in, the academies they were asked to found. Ignoring the prejudice that often surrounded them, they simply offered a solid education, bearing witness to God's love for all who came. Their diaries show us that they did so with humor as well as dedication, supported by faith and by the community of their sisters in New York and in Belgium.

Basing her story on diaries and letters, Sister St. John Begnaud, SSMN, tells something of the story from the point of view of the pioneer sisters, and in doing so helps us to see their faith, their courage, and their joy.

Those of us who were their students learned from the sisters the vocation we all have to a life of worship and service. They helped us understand St. Paul's insistence to Timothy, "God wants all people to be saved and to come to the knowledge of truth." They changed our lives, and probably yours.

>Monsignor Joseph Schumacher
>Former Vicar General of the Diocese of Fort Worth

Acknowledgments

Inadequate though it is, this story owes a debt to many people:

To Sister Louise Smith, without whom this effort would never have begun, would not have continued, and would surely not have been published. She harrowed our archives, harried her archivist friends, and, together with Sister Camella Menotti, rescued me from electronic challenges;

To Sister Patricia Ridgley, who gently prodded, and raised significant questions;

To Sister Cecile Faget, who encouraged, challenged, and patiently edited the text;

To Clarice Peninger, who painstakingly shepherded every word and comma;

To Sherrie Reynolds, who, out of her experience and her generosity, leapt over several barriers;

To Mary Gottschalk, whose skill and care added to this document a precision of detail it would otherwise never have known;

To the present community of Our Lady of Victory Convent, who patiently listened to stories, and who joined me in remembering;

To Mother Claire and Mother Emilie, who dared impossible enterprises in the "hope of doing a little good";

To Sister Mary Angela Healy, whose personal loss became gain for so many;

To each Sister of St. Mary of Namur, who, in her own way, has lived the charism that is the chalice for our gift to God:

In the simplicity of my heart, I have joyfully offered all to God.

Introduction

THE GOAL of this undertaking emerges clearly only as I continue writing. Its intended audience is the community of the Sisters of St. Mary of Namur, especially those in the Western Province, together with their Oblates, Associates, Auxiliary, former pupils, and friends.

As members of the Western Province of the Sisters of St. Mary of Namur, we are conscious of two realities:

- we bear the mark of our ancestors in the Congregation;
- as Texans, we have distinctive characteristics.

How did that come about? The heritage is received from our founders and those who have lived the charism of the Sisters of St. Mary within our memory, into our own lifetime. But as Texans we are recipients of a heritage that is not like that of others; a gift that must be lived here, in this place, if it is to be integrated into the living tradition of St. Mary. Each generation, each participant, must live it uniquely if it is to take its place in the tradition to be passed on to the future.

What I first attempt is to explore the force that drove ordinary people, and some extraordinary ones, to undertake enterprises that seemed impossible. Was there a pattern that was carried on from one generation, one foundation, to the next? Such a design can be traced only in hindsight. What I think we see is consistent:

> There are people who are not being offered the opportunity to hear the word of God. Obstacles are formidable.
>
> Someone dares to say, "We can't do much, but we can do something. Let's start here."
>
> A few people begin a project; it meets with some measure of success; others join the enterprise.
>
> As the group grows larger, someone becomes aware of another need, and proposes reaching out.
>
> There are differences of opinion; will a new project threaten the success of what we are doing here?
>
> Discussions are held; decisions are made. We will do this. Only a few will go, but the effort will be shared by all of us. Those who go will maintain contact; those who stay will offer prayer and support.
>
> The identity of the Congregation undergoes a major, though almost imperceptible, shift.

But the story does not end there. Those involved in the new enterprise encounter different circumstances. Things are not quite the way they were at home. Is it possible to be faithful both to what we have received and to what we experience here? Will the people back home understand? What changes must we make to enter into what God is doing here?

That pattern seems clear in the movement from Belgium to New York. It might seem less evident in the movement to Texas, since in it there is no new language to be acquired, no ocean to cross—though the train trip lasted nearly as long as an ocean voyage.

But the situation they found was different. The political atmosphere, the population, the climate were different. Fevers unknown in the North brought sickness, even early death. We find references made to the frontier mentality, to ox-drawn wagons, and to tent cities. The Civil War had wrought chaos to economic structures; the Reconstruction had destroyed structures of leadership; the Ku Klux Klan continued to spread hatred of Catholics as well as of Blacks.

As the small communities of Sisters of St. Mary dealt with these situations, something was changing in their understanding of themselves, of their Church, and of the Congregation to which they belonged. They themselves would change, and through them, the consciousness of the Congregation. It would happen slowly, sometimes painfully. Again and again the decision had to be made, at each level of relationship: Can we do this together?

It may help us to do this in our own day if we understand the early stages through which our history has passed. That is the purpose of this story.

1

Beginnings

"IT'S REALLY a rather unlikely event that the Sisters of St. Mary are celebrating almost 137 years in Texas," Sister Patricia Ridgley remarked as she reflected on her Congregation's history. "As a matter of fact, the Sisters of St. Mary *almost* didn't come to Texas, and once arrived they *almost* didn't stay." But come they did, and stayed, learning, as Sister Patricia puts it, that when you undertake a venture, you *"don't be too quick to turn back, and don't do it alone!"*

St. Paul, looking back on all he had done and forward to all he hoped to do, put it in other terms when he wrote to the Church in Rome: "All things work together for the good of those who love God" (Rom 8:28). Clearly God had prepared him, by education and ancestry as well as personal zeal, for a ministry he could not have foreseen. So the Sisters of St. Mary of Namur, looking back upon their history in Belgium, in New York, and in Texas, and looking forward to their hopes, have reason to echo St. Paul's assertion with personal conviction.

The improbabilities are there in history. The Congregation was established in Namur, Belgium, in 1819, when religious communities were forbidden throughout Belgium. Sisters of St. Mary would travel to New York in 1863, during the raging Civil War. Arriving in Texas in 1873 from Lockport, New York, they might have been labeled as despicable "carpetbaggers"! In each of these events, there seems to be a defiance of impossibility, but divine guidance is clear.

Their story opens in Belgium, a small country of northern Europe that remembers a chaotic history. Conquered by Julius Caesar, who described the inhabitants of that area as contentious, the area later knew Charlemagne and his immediate heirs as rulers. In the Middle Ages, the territory was marked by feudalism and then brought into centralization by the Dukes of Burgundy. Under Spanish rule in the sixteenth and seventeenth centuries (the territory was then known as Flanders), it was ruled by Austria in the eighteenth century, until the Brabant Revolution brought its people into the proud *Les États Belgique Unis* in 1790. That freedom, however, was short-lived, as the Austrian army retook power in December of 1790.

A victim of its strategic location, Belgium was bartered by more powerful neighbors. Belgians were not consulted when, in 1814–15, the Council of Vienna handed them over to the Prince of Orange, uniting them with the Netherlands, which were staunchly Protestant. Only forty years later, after another revolution, would the country gain political independence. Even then, it remained subject to the authority of larger nations as they sought a balance of power that might help them avoid conflict.

Reflecting, in his *Short History of Belgium*, on the many political changes, Dr. Léon Van Der Essen, Belgian historian and Professor at the University of Louvain, in 1920 commented: "The national culture of Belgium is a synthesis, where one finds the genius of two races, the Romance and the Germanic—mingled, yet modified by the imprint of the distinctively Belgian."[1] The resulting characteristics, in his opinion, are "a common desire for independence and freedom, a jealous regard for those popular rights which serve as a guaranty of independence and freedom, and a deeply religious spirit."[2]

It would seem that these characteristics can be traced in the history of the small religious congregation of Sisters of St. Mary that has its physical, spiritual, and psychological roots in Belgium. The physical roots are clear; the spiritual and

---

1. Van Der Essen, *Short History of Belgium*, 3.
2. Ibid., 4.

psychological influences seem no less evident in an overview of the Congregation's history.

Despite unfavorable circumstances, each new venture is marked by the regard for human rights, especially those of the marginalized. As the story unfolds, a certain pattern becomes evident:

> There is an unmet need.
> Resources to confront the need are inadequate.
> Someone nevertheless makes an audacious attempt to meet the need.
> Once begun, the effort draws others into the work.
> Against all probability, the effort succeeds.
> Within the community there arises passionate recognition of another need.
> The group ponders, discerns, authorizes outreach to new need, but without abandoning the current work; the entire community assumes responsibility for both.

The lesson Sister Patricia identifies is reinforced at each stage: When you start something, *don't turn back too soon, and don't do it alone.*

We may find the sequence first in our founder, Father Nicholas Joseph Minsart. As a young man, he fought in the Brabant Revolution. Though recognized for his courage and skill in battle, he did not envision a military career, but chose in 1790 to begin studies at Liège, and in the following year determined to offer his life to God as a monk. Entering the Cistercian Abbey of Boneffe, he became "Dom Jerome," and in 1793 was ordained a priest.

But the political destiny of his small country was not yet established. Annexation by France in 1795 brought intense persecution, as the aftermath of the French "Reign of Terror" forbade all religious practice, confiscated monasteries, and dispersed the religious who occupied them. The Lord's Day was not to be observed, nor were vows of religious life to be taken. A decree was passed against priests who refused to swear an oath of allegiance to the Civil Constitution of the Clergy; more than a thousand priests were assassinated in Paris prisons. The monks of Boneffe were scattered, and their monastery was taken over by the state. As the youngest member of his Cistercian community, Father Minsart naturally found his immediate and long-term destinies redirected.

French policy brought about the imprisonment of some of the monks, one of them an old man in fragile health. Dom Jerome offered to replace him, and was imprisoned for some months. Eventually freed, but now without a monastic home, Father Minsart joined other dispersed clergy in attempting to meet the spiritual needs of the persecuted people. There were secret gatherings of the former community. Though their situation was recognized as "precarious and dangerous," the priests administered the sacraments in secret, meeting, when they dared, in what they referred to as "our cave of mercy."[3]

Enter Napoleon Bonaparte, who in 1795 made Belgium once more a part of France. Though his policies reflected his desire for absolute power, he took a more tolerant approach to the relationship of church and state, even signing a concordat with Pope Pius VII in 1801. As priests returned to public ministry and Catholic worship was reestablished, Father John Devenise, a professor of Sacred Scripture and theology, was especially attentive to the young, who had grown up in such troubled times. Father Minsart, once his student, became his colleague.

In June of 1802, when the church bells of Namur rang out once more, the bishop of Namur reopened the seminary and named Father Devenise as rector. In 1806 Father Minsart, now a diocesan priest, joined Father Devenise in Namur and was named pastor of the church of St. John the Evangelist.

Namur, which is situated at the confluence of the Sambre and Meuse rivers, was at that time a walled city. The parish of St. Loup, at the heart of the poorest area, just below the fort called the "Citadel," was crowded and unhealthy. The presence of the five thousand soldiers quartered at the fort, as well as the activities of a distillery, several breweries, and numerous bars along the river, created an atmosphere

---

3. A Sister of Saint Mary of Namur, "Nicholas Joseph Minsart," 11.

that made Christian life difficult, especially for young women. Father Minsart sought ways to enable them to "earn an honest living."

Within his parish was a tailoring establishment owned by the Colson sisters.[4] Members of a once-aristocratic family, they now earned their living by their skills as seamstresses. Business was growing, and they employed several young women, among them Josephine Sana and Elisabeth Berger. Knowing that the group prayed as they worked, Father Minsart often passed by the shop to make prayer requests. He was not too surprised, then, when Josephine and Elisabeth spoke to him of their desire for religious life.

There was, of course, a problem. Religious congregations were still forbidden. There was no community to join. Undaunted, the pastor saw in their desire an act of Providence. Could they not respond to their calling by assuming the lifestyle of active religious, and in so doing meet the need of some of the desperate young women of the area? Sewing was a marketable skill. Together with basic catechism, it could prepare his parishioners to "earn an honest living." He would, when the need arose, develop a market for their skilled embroidery to help replace vestments destroyed in the Revolution.

---

4. Here, as in many other instances, the surviving records do not supply full names.

With contagious enthusiasm, he proposed the idea to the young women. He would supply a house—a simple structure one room wide, four stories tall. It would be their school, their workshop, and their residence. The highest room would be their chapel.

And so it happened. Though they could not be called religious sisters, Josephine Sana and Elisabeth Berger came together on November 11, 1819, in the small house provided by their pastor, and began to offer sewing lessons together with religious instruction to the young women of the area. They, and others who quickly joined them, became known as the "Pious Ladies of St. Loup," and the community quickly spread to other towns along the Sambre River. Parents soon asked that the girls be taught to read and write as well as sew, and thus began the tradition of Catholic education that continues to mark the Sisters of St. Mary of Namur on four continents even in the twenty-first century.

Because crowding and poverty made the area unhealthy, neither Josephine nor Elisabeth lived to pronounce vows when that was permitted in 1834; but among those who made commitment on that day was Rosalie Nizet, who is remembered in the Congregation as Mother Claire, the first superior general. (She was actually the second, but Catherine Roosen, who, as Sister Marie Thérèse, became the first general superior, died ten months after her religious profession.)

Rosalie doubtless needed a dispensation to enter the community, since canon law required that each candidate bring a dowry. That was a precaution against Europe's history of dispersing religious communities. In such event, a woman needed some resource to gain a foothold in the secular world. But Rosalie's resources were of another sort. "I can sew and cook and garden," she reported; and she expected to do just that in the community.

But Father Minsart was a good judge of character, and it was he who made appointments in the community. Sister Claire was named superior of the small group serving in Châtelet, where she used the skills she had claimed at her entrance. When it became clear in Namur that Sister Marie Thérèse was dying, Father Minsart asked Sister Claire to return to the motherhouse, and indicated to the sisters that she should become the next leader of the community. Consequently, it was Mother Claire, elected at the age of 26, who would preside over the spread of the community in Belgium, and eventually, in 1863, send Sisters of St. Mary to New York, witnessing to the missionary zeal that characterizes the Congregation.

Meanwhile, the situation in Belgium itself had changed. The Constitution of 1831 lifted the ban on religious congregations, allowing the return of traditional forms of religious life in Namur. Among the leaders of that movement was Father Minsart, who not only continued to nurture the small community he had formed, but brought other communities to the city. With the funds salvaged from the Abbey of Boneffe, he enabled the Brothers of Christian Schools to return to their ministry in Namur. (The favor was reciprocated: the brothers let him base the first Constitution of the Sisters of St. Mary on their Rule; and the vow formula used currently by the sisters is taken from that document.)

Nor was it only the brothers that profited from his support. Apparently serving as spiritual director to Mother Julie Billiart, he learned of her anxiety: her French bishop hesitated to allow her the freedom she needed to develop her young Congregation. She lamented the situation in a letter to Dom Minsart, and received this response: "You cannot disobey your bishop; but you can come here, where our bishop will support you." So became centered in the small Belgian city the community now known as the Sisters of Notre Dame de Namur. (Their motherhouse is very close to that of the Sisters of St. Mary of Namur.)

Father Minsart continued his attentiveness to Mother Claire's small group. Tradition tells us that it was his visit to a forest to select the wood to be used in the chapel of the Sisters of St. Mary that brought about the respiratory illness that took his life. That beautiful chapel, with minor renovations occasioned by liturgical change, is at the center of the large boarding school that stands on the site of our foundation. The current general council of the Congregation occupies modest quarters in the complex, and the sisters of the Belgian Province maintain contact with the school, which is now a flourishing and respected educational institution maintained by competent and dedicated laypersons in Namur.

The activity of the Congregation has spread to other areas. But in those early days, young women simply upon seeing the work being done by it in that one city came to join in it.

Pastors requested sisters to staff their growing schools. The Industrial Revolution had introduced the phenomenon of the "urban poor." Since small plots of land could no longer support a family, many moved to the towns developing around coal mines and factories. Men, women, and children worked long hours in difficult and often dangerous situations. The poor became a marketable commodity, used to make profits regardless of the human suffering involved.

Moved with compassion, Mother Claire and her community saw themselves as called especially to work in situations that involved the poor. Responding to an invitation to Rochefort, the Superior inquired about the work expected. "Be assured," replied the pastor, "it is the poor I will send to you." There, and in other early foundations, expenses were paid by benefactors, but the financial situation was always precarious. A special school was established in Mons to help towards self-sufficiency girls with very limited opportunities. There the sisters housed twelve orphans, who were also supported by benefactors. As Sister Patricia would later observe, neither religious nor laity "did it alone."

The archives of Sisters of St. Mary point out that the houses of Brugelette, La Bouverie, Fontaine-l'Evèque, and Huy opened in 1847—the same year "that Karl Marx launched his *Communist Manifesto*." The sisters saw another way of reaching out to the poor. At La Bouverie, we are told, "the sisters shared the poverty of the people they worked with, and, living alongside them, they brought a sense of dignity and self-worth into the lives of people who had become the victims of the early phase of the Industrial Revolution."[5]

Belgian pastors continued to send letters requesting more personnel. Twelve foundations were established between 1837 and 1868. By choice these were in the most heavily industrialized areas, mostly along the Sambre River.

But Mother Claire was alert to the changing world. Across the ocean, new frontiers were opening. A young man from the Flemish section of Belgium had also sensed a vocation to spread God's word. Pierre De Smet had entered the seminary at

---

5. Historical note; SSMN archives, Namur.

the age of fourteen, and six years later had traveled to the United States to enter the Jesuit novitiate in Maryland. Sent in 1838 to found a mission among the Potawatomi Indians, he began to keep journals and to write long letters about his experiences. The documents wakened in many the call to mission. Belgian awareness was intensified when Father De Smet visited the country of his birth to recruit help in his very extensive mission. Early in 1861 he spoke personally with Mother Claire, inviting her community to share his ministry. Word spread rapidly among the sisters.

Some were eager to go, but all were excitedly involved. "Surely," they said among themselves, "we can send some sisters to America. The rest of us will work hard to handle needs here." Enthusiasm spread, and discussion was lively.

2

Decisions

Hope was high. On his visit to Namur early in 1861, Father De Smet had offered a plan as well as an invitation. A large plot of land was available near St. Louis, where the sisters would assist him in his work among the Native Americans. He would procure "a suitable establishment" for the sisters Mother Claire would send to America.[1]

But in the U.S., civil war broke out. What effect would that have on the project? After months of waiting for news, Mother Claire wrote the Jesuit priest on October 17, 1862:

> Since the interview I had with you on 10 March, my council and I have examined the project relating to the foundation of our Institute in America. This project seems advantageous to us for many reasons, and so we would like to see it realized in the near

---

1. SSMN archives, Buffalo, NY.

> future. Several of our sisters would be very happy to be sent to this far-off mission, and each day they pray heaven to accord them this joy. It seems to them they could work more profitably for the glory of God and the good of souls in an American city rather than in a Belgian one. Belgium is well supplied with excellent educational institutions, so parents have no difficulty in finding schools in which their children may be brought up in the Christian faith.[2]

The phrase "the glory of God and the good of souls" recurs often in the literature of the time, reflecting the strong influence of the Jesuits on the Belgian community. Situated close to the cathedral of Namur and very near the motherhouse of St. Mary, they served as chaplains, confessors, and retreat directors for the sisters, even working with Mother Claire on the Institute's Constitution. For that reason she would make serious efforts to ensure that the sisters she would send on mission would be under their direction in the New World. She continues explaining to Father De Smet: "The foundation of a house in the United States would, by enlarging the number of our works, permit us to receive a greater number of novices. It would reanimate in our sisters a spirit of zeal and generosity and be to all a most efficacious means of corresponding to our holy vocation."[3]

2. Ibid.
3. Ibid.

Clearly, the few who would be sent would not be alone. Their understanding of their part in community is evident in the correspondence written during their troubled voyage. To say that they were homesick is an understatement; that they understood their mission not simply as their own, but as that of their religious family, is no less clear. It is a heritage reflected in the present Constitution of the Sisters of St. Mary, which speaks of the "consultation and dialogue" by which the sisters "seek the best way for each one to serve in response to the needs recognized."

In that early letter to Father De Smet, Mother Claire explains that she and her council have also considered the invitation of the vicar apostolic of Bombay to serve in India. After discussing that proposal with the bishop of Namur, all agreed that "communication with that country would be too hazardous and expensive," so that the focus on America was definitive. Having said that, she comes straight to the point, asking, "May the Sisters of St. Mary hope to establish themselves in the United States? If so, when? Where? Under what conditions?"[4]

The reply was another six months in coming. Father De Smet explained that the delay was due to the war, which he described in some detail: because of the violent struggle, hospitals were full to overflowing, schools were closed, many people were

4. Ibid.

out of work and in great need. In a time of peace, the sisters would surely have received several invitations from bishops, but in the present situation the project should be delayed; not abandoned.

This news brought great disappointment to the would-be missionaries. But Father De Smet was aware of their eagerness. In a visit to his friend Bishop John Timon, of the Buffalo Diocese, he spoke of the Belgian community so eager to come to America. Having long wanted to have European sisters for his diocese, the bishop showed an interest that Father De Smet communicated to Mother Claire. Her response was prompt. Writing to Bishop Timon, she explains: "A few days ago I had a letter from Father De Smet . . . which gives me hope that our project will at last be realized, and that it is to your diocese and under your paternal direction that Divine Providence calls us."[5] Within a year "from this date," she continues, she should be able to place at his disposal six sisters, four of whom will be for teaching, and two for domestic work. "Two," she says, "are able to speak and teach English, French, and German; the others know French and English. There are many eager and zealous young religious who would be eager to serve as the mission developed."

Financial resources were less promising. The community would be unable to do more than pay

---

5. SSMN archives, Buffalo.

the passage of those who would go to America. They could offer them no support after their arrival. Bishop Timon replied that finances in his diocese were also limited, but he would be able to supply a house for the sisters; and, he added, he was sure that "the good people of Belgium will aid you as they have helped many missionary enterprises in the New World." (He knew whereof he spoke, having served as a missionary in Texas and other states in his earlier years.) Again the sisters would serve as a bridge between donors and recipients.

With those rather indefinite promises, the project moved forward. We know from some writings and from oral tradition that the sisters' ability to speak English was more limited than they realized, and that the house they found upon their arrival was hardly what they were expecting!

But those were concerns for the future. The first question was who would be sent; and most importantly, who would be charged with responsibility for directions taken by the group so distant from the motherhouse and confronted by unprecedented situations.

Looking back, we see Sister Emilie as a natural choice. We read that as a child, Josephine Kemen, along with her brother Jules, was intrigued by stories of Native Americans and dreamed of bringing them to God. Their plan was simple: "Jules would evangelize, administer Baptism, say Mass and convert souls, and Josephine would instruct the little savages and prepare them for their First Communion. They resolved to be very good, to pray well, and to study diligently so as to be able later to accomplish their beautiful mission: to save souls for God."[6]

It was not surprising that the children should have such ambitions; they came of a deeply religious family. Their Prussian grandfather had suffered harsh imprisonment for sheltering a Dominican nun during the time of persecution. His possessions had been confiscated and his wife forced to flee with their infant. Eventually reunited, the once prosperous family came to know unfamiliar poverty. The experience strongly influenced their five children, deepening family bonds. Mary Anne, the youngest, remained at home for many years to care for her invalid mother. Only after that death did she ask admission to the Sisters of St. Mary, where she became Sister Aline—the first gift of a family that would, in the next generation, offer three members to the Congregation.

But there were marriages too. Mary Anne's sister, Marie-Madeleine, married John Adam Kemen, and of that union were born Josephine, Jules, and their five siblings.

On May 1, 1844, the twenty-year-old Josephine entered the Sisters of St. Mary. On July 23, 1844, she received the habit of the community and took the

---

6. A Sister of St. Mary of Namur, "Life of Mother Emilie," 7.

name Sister Emilie of St. Cecilia. After being admitted to first vows in 1846, she served at the motherhouse as a teacher of religion, art, and German. Her personal piety, excellent education, and qualities of leadership were recognized in her eventual appointment as Director of Novices and her later one as Assistant to the General Superior. It was from the latter position that she was called to lead the small band that would undertake the mission to America.

In our days of e-mail and Skype, it is hard to imagine the responsibility that appointment involved. Traditionally, the chain of authority was clear: certain decisions were to be made by the General Superior alone; others required consent of her council. But decisions in America would have to be based on judgment of situations there. Who would make those decisions for a people of a different language, a different culture, a different social, political, and religious mindset? The new situation would require, on the one hand, a profound trust on the part of those sending, and on the other, a deep sense of community on the part of those sent. Only that double bond would preserve the unity of the Institute while allowing it to adjust to its new situation.

The band that Mother Emilie would lead was not of a single cultural background.[7] Herself Prussian by birth, she was joined by Sister Mary Claver Van Lint, Sister Mary of St. Joseph Cary, Sister Augustine of the Cross Barry, and Sister Paula Tischenbach. Among the five of them, four countries were represented: Germany, Belgium, Luxembourg, and Ireland. Possibly it is only from Belgium, and from that particular period of its history, that such a disparate group might emerge.

Christine Van Lint, "trained in voice under Wilbrant, one of the best teachers of music in Europe," was expected to have a brilliant career in opera.[8] When, at age nineteen, she announced her intention to enter a religious community, Wilbrant joined her family and her admirers in trying to dissuade her. Her perseverance as Sister Mary Claver brought to the Sisters of St. Mary in America the tradition of love for music and the arts.

Catherine Cary, who would become Sister Mary of St. Joseph, had been born in Luxembourg, and educated in France, England, and Italy. Her competency was sorely challenged in her role as treasurer of the new foundation, where there was little money to manage!

---

7. Having access to few primary sources for the section concerning the Lockport foundation, the author depends for dialogue and for some names on Sister Mary Louise Corcoran's book, *Seal of Simplicity*, which tells that story. Copyright privilege has been granted.

8. Corcoran, *Seal of Simplicity*, 86.

Sister Augustine (formerly Arabella) Barry had come from Ireland as a child to study with the Sisters of St. Mary in Namur. As the only native English speaker of the group, she was of special importance, though it is written that Mother Emilie reproached her for her timidity in asking questions in the new environment, where she herself found her formal education inadequate in face of the varied accents and usage that surrounded her in America.

A native of Luxembourg, Sister Paula (formerly Elizabeth) Tischenbach was assigned the important role of housekeeper and cook. To establish a home in the new environment must have been a special challenge to her.

As they left Namur on the seventh of August, 1863, they must have been very conscious that they were leaving behind much that was dear. Most would never again see their families, or the sisters with whom they had shared so much life experience. Their commitment to God and their Rule, their small community, and their sense of mission were all they had.

The *seal of simplicity* leads them on each step of their journey: by train to Brussels, accompanied by two other sisters; the next day, on to Antwerp, where they waved a final farewell as the *Dolphin* lifted anchor. Morning found them in London, where they were met by Mother Emilie's brother Charles, who was then teaching at Oscott College.

A cart was needed to transport the sisters' "voluminous baggage" to the next train. What, we might wonder, was in the baggage? (One record says that altar linens and vestments were included.) How does one pack for an indefinite stay in an unknown country? What will be needed there, and what will be available? That concern would be for the future, the sisters thought as they boarded the train that took them to Holywell, in Wales.

There they were to meet two Jesuit priests—Fathers Cornelius Smarius and William Becker—and two Capuchin friars. It was Father Smarius who would accompany the sisters, first on their train trip to Liverpool, then on their long voyage across the ocean. Such was the confusion in the Liverpool station that the sisters "transferred three times to different vessels" (each time, presumably, with their luggage!); but they arrived a few hours later at Queenstown, where they boarded the *City of Baltimore*.

A pleasant surprise awaited them there. A small boat arrived with friends they had known in Namur: the Healys, the Hogans, the O'Connells, and the Barrys; thirty-one well-wishers, loaded with gifts. More luggage! But these were unexpected luxuries: wines, fruit, and candy, as well as stationery, crochet hooks, and thread. It was a good thing that the fruit included lemons, since by the next day all but Sister Mary Claver were seasick! Only she was able to serve the patients the lemonade Father Smarius prepared for them! Apparently seasickness was an unfamiliar ailment, since Sister Mary of St. Joseph gave a detailed account of it in a letter home.

> "Besides experiencing a complete languor of the whole body," she explained, "one is not able to take a drop of water or to make the least movement without paying tribute to the inexorable god of the sea. On land one can secure some relief, but on sea everything is against you: a bed that turns without ceasing; a cabin where windows remain closed so that the waves will not dash in; an odor of tar and the sound of machinery tormenting the senses."[9]

On Saturday, August 15, the patronal feast day of the Institute, they experienced a particularly violent storm. Those who attempted to move were "dashed against beds or hurled on the floor." They must have dreamed of the beautiful celebration taking place in Namur, but Sister Mary Claver summarized their own experience by what she wrote in the diary: "Rain, wind, rough sea."

By August 18, a calm sea allowed for music on deck. The soul of the musician responded with delight: "Nothing is so lovely as a concert on the water. The sweet harmony seems to cast a magic spell over the very waves."

9. Ibid., 94.

The spell did not hold, however. By morning the violence of the waves was such that it took use of both steam and sail to control the vessel. The captain directed the ship towards Cape Race, a fact that terrified those aware of the icebergs in that area. The storm lasted for eighteen seemingly endless hours. The captain's adjustment of direction sent the ship to the coast of Newfoundland, where a cold morning found Sister Mary Claver sitting on deck, journal in hand. She recalls watching the fishing boats, and then having her attention directed by the captain to a huge whale. It was an awesome experience. That evening she also writes: "The sun is a red globe of fire plunging down into a dark sea, with water and sky reflecting crimson. Everyone is enjoying this sight predicting good weather." All was well; the ship was scheduled to dock in New York on August 23.

That hope, however, was soon dashed. Evidently drawn from the journal's account, Sister Mary Louise's is frighteningly vivid:

> No one expected another storm, but it came. Its indescribable fury made their former experience fade into insignificance. The wind swelled the sails, making it impossible to fold them; the vessel plunged, heaved, and reared as the winds lashed and roared, tossing monstrous, billowing waves mountain high, seemingly ready to engulf the ship. A terrifying, grinding, deafening noise, like a sinister herald, seemed to

announce that the ship was being dashed against the rocks.[10]

Ever attentive to the small community, Father Smarius urged the sisters to return to their cabin and "offer up some prayers: first the *Memorare*, and then the beads," and said reassuringly, "I'll soon be back." But when he returned, his face was grave. "Sisters," he said, "prepare for death. No doubt our Lady can save us, for she is all-powerful. But if it is God's will that we be buried at sea, then let us be resigned." He promised to give general absolution.[11]

What must have been their thoughts? Beyond the terror of the tossing ship, and the thought of the wild, cold water, must have been the question, Is this how it is to end?

What was God saying? After the months of planning, the joy of being chosen, the sadness of parting, was it all to end here, in the unmarked grave of the sea?

Their journal speaks of "indescribable terror" in face of the power of the sea. At midnight Father Smarius reported that nothing had changed. Until about 4:30 a.m., they felt themselves suspended between life and death. Then, when the storm abated, they could say, "God be praised! Sweet Star of the Sea, refuge of the afflicted, you have heard your children's prayer!"

10. Ibid., 96.
11. Ibid.

At daybreak they were told that they would be in New York the following day. At ten that night the ship sailed into the bay, under a full moon. The *City of Baltimore* released a series of fireworks, reminding the sisters of "a fete at home." What a great welcome to America!

Father Smarius was there to guide them through customs and to summon cabs to take them to the Jesuit college. Doubtlessly relieved to have brought them safely to land, Father Smarius introduced the weary travelers to his confreres as "Jesuit nuns." He accompanied them to Fordham University, where they were introduced to the Jesuit Provincial Superior. Their first night was spent with the Religious of the Sacred Heart. After the bustle of landing and of introductions, they were probably relieved to learn that those sisters were in retreat. Their English would not be tested that evening.

Father Smarius promised to take them the next morning to Lockport; but he proved too ill, perhaps too exhausted, to make the trip. With him vanished the last trace of contact with home! Father Becker directed the sisters to the station, where they boarded the train.

Alone in a totally unfamiliar country, and surrounded by a language that must have sounded like Babel, they experienced another crisis. Unsure of their situation, unable to ask questions, they could only hope that the train would take them to their destination. How far was it? Who would welcome them? How would they know what to do?

We are unsure of how the "voluminous baggage" kept up with them on the several stages of their journey. The train they had boarded in New York followed the valley of the Hudson River. When it stopped at nightfall, the sisters got off; they followed the crowd to the ferry that made the crossing to Albany. Again they alighted. What were they to do now?

We can only guess what this uncertainty meant to Mother Emilie, an educated woman, daughter of an aristocratic family, a person used to making decisions, to exercising authority. Unable even to ask questions, she turned to the Irish-born Sister Augustine, who had come to Belgium as a child. Surely she . . . but she had spoken little English as an adult; timid by nature, and overcome by the unfamiliar surroundings, she dared not inquire.

Nevertheless, they stumbled along together and found themselves seated on the train bound first for Rochester, then for Lockport. Soon they would be in their new home. They would relax, pray, rid themselves of the outmoded clothes they had worn for the journey, and don their habits. They would be prepared to meet their pastor.

But culture shock was only beginning. In Lockport, the stationmaster came to tell them that their trunks had arrived the evening before. Otherwise unmet, Mother Emilie called a carriage and asked to be taken to the rectory near St. John's Church. Aware that Bishop Timon was in Buffalo, they hoped only to meet their new pastor, whose name they had not been told.

"I'll get our key from the priest," Mother Emilie told the others. But it was not to be. When the carriage stopped before a small house next to an old church, she asked the driver to request the key from the priest. Walking through the unkempt yard, he knocked on the door and asked for the priest, but it was the housekeeper who came to the carriage, and a rather shabby housekeeper she was. To the European sisters, accustomed to splendid churches even where the people were poor; whose experience was of a society in which classes were clearly distinguished, and Church personnel were high in rank, the scene must have been appalling. The conversation was hardly less so.

Turning to Sister Augustine, whose English was better than her own, Mother Emilie told her to request the key to their house. The reply was unbelievable.

"This is your house."

"Is this the priest's house?"

"Yes, it is."

"But where is the house for the sisters?"

"This is the house for the sisters."

"For the priest too?"

"Yes, of course it's for the priest too."[12]

Surely, Mother Emilie must have thought, there was some mistake. The priest, when he would come, would set things right. They followed the housekeeper into an unimpressive room. Faded wallpaper, battered furniture, general disorder characterized their surroundings.

The priest, when he arrived with pipe in mouth and carriage whip in hand, was hardly more conventional. "Are you the sisters?" he inquired hesitantly. (They still had on the lay clothes they had been advised to wear for the journey.)

Mother Emilie's response was textbook-correct: "Yes, sir. And to whom have we the honor of speaking?"

"I am Father Gleason."

Again the textbook reply: "We are glad to make your acquaintance."

"Thank you. How are you? Did you have a pleasant trip?"

"It was quite stormy, Father. We would be very glad if you would show us the house where we are to live. We could not make the maid understand us."

"It's right here," Father Gleason said, as if he were explaining the obvious.

"Here?" Mother Emilie had glimpsed, from the front entrance, the four rooms of the first floor.

---

12. Ibid., 102.

There must be some mistake. "But surely we cannot establish classrooms here."

"There is more room here than you will need!" said Father Gleason, laughing. And with that he walked off, calling out, "Ann, get them something to eat!" End of conversation.

The story goes on in vivid detail: An attempt to lock the door through which the "voluminous luggage" had been brought in revealed the fact that that door had no lock. Hastily the sisters opened the trunk that contained their habits. Perhaps proper attire would restore some measure of normalcy. They dressed quickly as they heard their pastor running down the stairs "chanting in a fine baritone" Psalm 114 ("When Israel came forth from Egypt . . ."). Their new life was beginning.

Led to the dining room, they were appalled at its condition. Anyone who has known the "godly cleanliness" of a Belgian convent can imagine their response to a dirty tablecloth, and to water served in glasses marked with fingerprints not their own. The soup was to their taste, but eggs, potatoes, and "black caudle" were prepared in ways that seemed to them unfit for human consumption; the much-desired coffee was unrecognizable. What could they say? How would they live?

But live they did, and acquired a deep respect for the Irish priest who sang psalms while running up or down the stairs ("so unlike our dignified

Belgian priests"), who assured them that they could start a school in the church basement they did not know existed, but found filthy and furnished only with benches. Drawing on her experience, Mother Emilie wisely withheld judgment. "I will have to know him better," she said. "He is a zealous priest, I am sure. Sisters, we must be a greater source of annoyance to him than he is to us. We do not understand each other, that is all." And so the sisters cleaned vigorously, because that was their tradition; they prayed fervently, because that was their faith; and they welcomed children, because that was what they had come to do.

The people they served were a largely immigrant population, predominantly German and Irish. Bishop Timon and Father Gleason clearly identified with the Irish community, but a German priest, Father Joseph Zoegel, also became a friend of the community. Mother Emilie enjoyed conversations with him in their native language. The diverse backgrounds of the sisters must have been an advantage as they worked to build bridges. Seriously persecuted by the anti-immigrant, anti-Catholic political party of Know-Nothings, the Catholic community could ill afford divisions.

Wonderful stories of those early days are told in *Seal of Simplicity*, from which much of the above has been shamelessly plagiarized (community property!). In later letters Mother Emilie would write,

"We made many mistakes," and "If I had known the American mentality, I would have understood much better." Like all other well-meaning immigrants, they struggled on, coming to love the people they served.

But other bridges too were needed. Coming to America from class-conscious Europe and a Belgian population that defined itself as Catholic, the sisters faced a crisis of relationship with the motherhouse. How would superiors there understand the new situation? Receiving authorization for purchase of property or adaptation of the Rule required weeks, and it could happen that the situation had changed before permissions arrived. But bonds were strong, especially among the first generation of missionaries. They would be tested over the years.

3

From Ireland to Texas

WHATEVER DIFFICULTIES the pioneer missionaries experienced, the spread of their work gives witness to their adaptation, and once more the pattern is repeated. From the troubled beginnings, new growth takes place. American girls as well as immigrants enter the novitiate. The work in Lockport comes to include schools that charge tuition and others that do not. One school served the Irish population, another the German. Schools were founded in Aurora, Elmira, Kenmore, and Buffalo; the sisters would go to Lowell, Massachusetts; eventually the province would establish missions in South Carolina and Georgia. That story is well told in *Seal of Simplicity*. But our goal here is to move toward the totally new step, the expansion to Texas.

On the surface, the story is simple: the sisters in Lockport received an invitation from the bishop of Galveston to establish a boarding school in his diocese. But why these sisters? And why that diocese? To appreciate God's work in that invitation, we need to visit its scattered origins: a young mother who died in Ireland, a Catholic judge in Corpus Christi who married a woman orphaned by that death, and a bishop who had ridden the plains of Texas when it held no priest, rectory, or convent.

First, the tragic death of an Irish mother, Jane Healy, who left four children: Margaret Mary, age 5; Thomas, 4; Richard, 3; and a baby girl called Jennie.[1] Their father, Dr. Richard Healy, together with Dr. Barry (a close relative of their mother), ran a hospital in Cahirciveen, Ireland. The children's maternal aunts, Mary and Johanna Murphy, stepped in to care for the children after their mother's death.

Conditions in Ireland became less and less tolerable following upon the Act of Union. Having declared England and Ireland one country, the English imposed heavy taxes and oppressive laws, bringing dire poverty to the Irish. In 1839 the Healy aunts, together with two uncles, John and Walter Murphy, set out for Virginia, taking with them their nephews Thomas and Richard Healy. They soon settled on a farm in West Virginia. Jennie did not go to America, but was sent to boarding school in Namur, where she had a cousin: Sister Augustine Barry, of the Sisters of St. Mary. Margaret Mary refused to leave

---

1. Material concerning the Murphy family is taken primarily from Sister Mary Immaculata Turley, SHG, *Mother Margaret Mary Healy-Murphy*.

her father, and in 1845 he took her with him on an "ill-equipped emigrant ship" bound for America. Food being scarce and the conditions unhealthy, many died on the voyage. Once landed in Freeport, Virginia, Dr. Healy experienced a period of exhaustion that caused delay in joining their relatives already established in West Virginia.

When finally they were able to make the rough overland journey, the family rejoiced in once more being together. Here, however, they encountered not only bigotry, but also the absence of a Catholic church and its ministers. Troubled by this lack, they decided to move southward, arriving eventually at New Orleans, where they found a house near St. Patrick's Church. Dr. Healy died there.

The family's final goal was Texas, where land was cheap and immigrants were welcome. Delayed by a border dispute with Mexico, they eventually moved, under the protection of the army of occupation, to Matamoros, where they established a hotel. Frontier settlements, however, were in continual flux. Walter Murphy joined the California Gold Rush in 1849, taking with him his nephews, Thomas and Richard. Walter died en route, of yellow fever. The nephews, brothers of Margaret Mary and Jennie, were never heard from again. The second uncle, John Murphy, died from the bullet of a fleeing bandit as he and Margaret sat on their patio. Margaret Mary was left alone with her aunts.

But other Irish immigrants were also looking toward Texas as a land of opportunity, and through that movement we meet another person crucial to the Waco foundation of the Sisters of St. Mary. John Bernard Murphy (not related), a gifted and ambitious young immigrant, became a close friend of the Healy family. Not surprisingly, he was attracted to Margaret Mary, whom he married on her sixteenth birthday: May 4, 1849.

Their story is typical of married life on the frontiers of Texas in the nineteenth century. John Murphy was an enterprising young man who learned the skills needed to be a real estate agent, stockman, lawyer, politician, and judge, as well as general entrepreneur. When a demographic shift weakened the success of the hotel he had bought, he invested in a ranch; and with his wife he established a home in San Patricio, in a colony of Irish-born professional persons. Throughout his economic success, his wife was noted for her care for the poor.

John Murphy had developed both a significant law practice and a recognition as one interested in government. (He was known as an active participant in the Constitutional Convention of Texas.) The family purchased a home in Corpus Christi, a town once prosperous, but at this period devastated by war. When the yellow fever epidemic of 1867 broke out, Margaret Mary Healy Murphy redoubled her efforts to serve the sick, especially the poor. Among the patients she cared for was a Mrs. Delaney, whose only concern as she was dying was that her small daughter, Minnie, would be left alone. The Murphys took the child into their home when the mother died, and it was through her that the history of the Sisters of St. Mary of Namur took a new turn, and two strands of history intertwined.

Throughout the years, Margaret Mary maintained contact with her younger sister, Jennie, who after graduation had entered the Sisters of St. Mary in Namur and taken the name Sister Mary Angela. She too was now in America, having come with the second group of missionaries. The reunion of Margaret Mary and Jennie must have been very special, since there is no record that the two sisters had seen each other since they were separated as children.

Diaries tells us that the Murphys visited Lockport in 1869 to bring their adopted daughter to be educated with the Sisters of St. Mary, and that they spoke of the need for Catholic schools in Texas. Their influence has long been recognized. What is not well documented, though it is held in tradition and noted in *Seal of Simplicity*, is the role of Bishop John Timon, of Buffalo, who died in 1867, two years before the first recorded visit of the Murphys. "Go to Texas and it's yours," he is reported to have said to Mother Emilie. What might have been the occasion for that conversation? Mother Emilie's letters speak frequently of Bishop Timon's "fatherly concern" for the now-growing Sisters of St. Mary. It is highly probable, then, that he visited the community when the second group of missionaries arrived from Belgium in 1865. Might not Sister Mary Angela have mentioned her sister who lived in Corpus Christi, and would not such a remark have brought Bishop Timon to recall his own experiences there?

We know that Timon returned several times to Texas even after moving to Buffalo, but much of his early experience of the state took him through the more developed towns of South Texas, where he reported that the faith was very much alive, especially among the Spanish-speaking population. A later exploration is shared with his Assistant Prefect Apostolic, later Bishop John Odin, CM, who reported tornadoes, as well as Indians raiding Texas ranchos and attacking travelers. Odin tells too of a cholera epidemic, of the absence of shade trees as he rode horseback across the state, of "scalding heat" and "brackish water" such that "we were happy if we found a little hole where we disputed with the frogs for a few drops of dirty, disgusting water." On July 24, 1825, his diary reports:

> God watches over us with such paternal care and goodness that no accident has yet occurred; frequently my horse has fallen; the branches of trees could many times have endangered my life; serpents, which

> abound almost everywhere, are often between the legs of my horse; bears have fled before me, and amidst all these perils, nothing serious has ever befallen me.[2]

Timon surely remembered those experiences. Nevertheless, according to historian James Talmadge Moore, Timon's report on Texas at that early stage was a "cautiously optimistic" one conveying that "there was much potential for the Catholic Church in Texas . . . , but the best missionaries possible must be sent, men able to withstand adverse conditions and able to inspire the highest public confidence."[3]

Undoubtedly memories of both the needs and the difficulties of his early ministry remained in his pastoral concern and might well have entered into his conversation with Mother Emilie.

Whatever Bishop Timon's comments might have been, we know that the Murphys, in the course of the family visit, explained the need for Catholic schools in the frontier settlements of Texas. Though the Church in South Texas had experienced early development, the devastation of the border wars and then of the Civil War had brought serious damage. Former slaves, who had received no preparation for independent life, were angry, restless, and sometimes violent. Children of any but the wealthiest families remained illiterate, roaming the streets.

---

2. James Talmadge Moore, *Through Fire and Flood*, 35.
3. Ibid., 21.

Could not the Sisters of St. Mary send missionaries to the South?

The request was addressed to the new superior general, Mother Delphine Marx, who saw no way of responding to it. The Belgian community had established thirteen schools in their own country. The New York group, not yet a province, struggled to support its several schools in Lockport. Further expansion could endanger the stability of what already existed.

But John Murphy knew how to get things done! The appropriate level of authority in Belgium must be addressed by the same level of authority in Texas. With the support of Bishop Claude Marie Dubuis of Galveston, whose diocese included the whole of Texas, Murphy begged Mother Delphine to contact Bishop Théodore-Joseph Gravez of Namur, who, as the ecclesiastical superior of the Institute, readily consented to the project. Bishop Stephen Vincent Ryan of Buffalo also blessed the venture, and so preparations were made to open a school in Texas.

They must have expected new experiences, but did they realize that the new venture would challenge their concepts of space and of time? Texas is a state the size of France, a territory scarcely imaginable to citizens of the small European country; but Belgians could boast an awareness of long history. The European sisters who sought a mission in Texas had seen the medieval and Renaissance churches that were the pride of European cities. The situation in Texas would surely challenge their imagination.

What, then, could have attracted the sisters to the South? Did they have any idea of the prejudice that awaited them there? The Murphys must have been very persuasive. But there were also reasons internal to the community. Young immigrants and native-born Americans were entering the novitiate. The book of "Entrance Information for the American Province" lists twenty-six women who entered the Lockport novitiate between 1865 and 1875. Among them, we know the story of Irish-born Sister Agnes Connolly (see below, "Personal Stories"), who was destined not only to serve in Texas, but eventually to be buried there. Once more it was time to "set out together," as Prussian and Irish, Belgian and Luxembourgois had done a scarce ten years before. This time there was Mother Emilie, a native of Prussia; Sister Mary Angela, born of an Irish mother in Bristol, England, and educated in Belgium;[4] and young Sister Stanislaus (formerly Elizabeth Eagan), American-born.

The Murphys would surely have preferred South Texas, an area more immediately accessible to them, with well-established Catholic institutions. But the sisters had different criteria. Central Texas had as yet no resident priest and no school. With the state's independence from Mexico, the bishop

---

4. School record; SSMN archives, Namur.

of Monterrey no longer held jurisdiction in the new Republic, nor had a new diocese been announced. In 1837 a group of Irish colonists had addressed a letter to the Third Provincial Council of Baltimore (the United States having been the first nation to recognize Texan independence) requesting that they send English-speaking priests to Texas, though most Texas Catholics spoke Spanish.[5] Their letter acknowledged that to be a priest in Texas would be "fatiguing and arduous," since Catholics were scattered over a vast area and were often poor.

In his earlier explorations, Father Timon had reported that Texas was ripe for evangelization. By mid-nineteenth century, much progress had been made. Ursulines arriving from Europe had established the first Catholic school in the port city of Galveston in 1847, and St. Mary's Cathedral had been dedicated in 1848. St. Mary's College was founded in San Antonio, and St. Mary's Seminary in Galveston, in 1852. The Sisters of Divine Providence had set up schools in several villages, and the Sisters of Charity of the Incarnate Word had an orphanage in San Antonio. Religious establishments, like commercial ventures, were for the most part in the southern area of the state, since Europeans usually entered Texas via the port city of Galveston and did not venture farther north than Austin before the railroad came. Though the Civil War had devastated

---

5. Moore, 10.

the area (federal forces occupied Galveston in 1865), and the harsh policies of Reconstruction had introduced questionable leadership, there was a recognizable presence of the Church in the southern area of the state.

Was that a factor in Mother Emilie's preference for a different area? Word had spread quickly that the railway system now served the area farther north. The sisters would go where people were more in need of faith support. The enterprise did not seem impossible to the sisters in New York. Texas was, after all, a state of the Union; the same language was spoken, the same flag was flown. But Texas would prove different.

Settled by people of European origin only in the mid-nineteenth century, the Village of Waco had been recognized by the United States and dignified with its first post office only in 1850; incorporation came in 1856. Very much a frontier town, it must have been shocking to those who remembered the streets of Namur, which are paved in centuries of history. (The citadel that overlooks Namur was used as a fort by the forces of Julius Caesar!) The suspension bridge that crossed the Brazos River had been completed only in 1870, and the first train came to Waco in 1871.

The population was predominantly Protestant. At that time, each nation of Europe had an established religion, and Mexico, like Spain, had been rooted in Catholicism. Because that government had been seen as oppressive (especially by Protestants who had declared themselves Catholic in order to obtain land), the newly independent Texas nurtured unhappy memories of the Church.

Already in New York, the sisters had encountered problems with the Nativists. The fact that the head of the Catholic Church lived in Rome set on edge the teeth of those who wanted America to be its own center. Mother Emilie had written that the sisters were criticized because they were loyal to Namur. As a further problem, these sisters came to Texas from north of the Mason–Dixon Line at the end of the oppressive period of Reconstruction! Add to those problems the presence in Texas of the Ku Klux Klan, which openly hated Catholics and Blacks! It was not a promising situation.

Though Waco had not been the scene of Civil War battles, it had been deeply troubled by the struggle. According to *Handbook of Texas Online* contributor Roger N. Conger, "many of the town's most prominent citizens sympathized with the Southern secessionist cause. . . . Seventeen companies of Confederate soldiers were raised from Waco and the surrounding countryside, and six Confederate generals were from the town."[6] Another *Handbook* contributor, Richard B.

---

6. Conger, "Waco, TX," para. 3; http://www.tshaonline.org/handbook/online/articles/hdwo1 (accessed September 10, 2011).

McCaslin, tells us that when rumors spread that a secret Union group was plotting revolt, "Texas state troops led by Col. James G. Bourland arrested more than 150 men on the morning of October 1 [1862]. . . . The military achieved its goal of eliminating the leadership of the Union League in Cooke County when the jury condemned seven influential Unionists, but an angry mob took matters into its own hands and lynched fourteen more before the jurors recessed."[7] Clearly, Texas was not a bastion of tolerance.

Nor was it known for tranquil beauty. Because the town was on a spur of the Chisholm Trail, says Conger, "by 1871 between 600,000 and 700,000 cattle had been driven through the town." Only when the suspension bridge was completed in 1870 was the "Village" incorporated as the "City of Waco."[8] Hardly surprising is Conger's report that "the town had many saloons and gaming houses during the 1870s, attracting cowhands, drifters, and others who helped earn the town the nickname of 'Six Shooter Junction.'"

It was to this "City" that three sisters came, hoping, in the words of Mother Emilie, to "do a little good." Having arrived by train in what would later be known as East Waco, they were met at the

7. McCaslin, "Great Hanging at Gainesville," para. 4; http://www.tshaonline.org/handbook/online/articles/jig01 (accessed September 10, 2011).

8. Conger, "Waco, TX," para. 4.

station, and driven across the then-famous suspension bridge that linked the two parts of the city. After spending the first night in a hotel, they were driven several blocks the next day to their home, located diagonally across from the newly founded St. Mary's Church of the Assumption (at Sixth and Washington). There they found a structure of four small rooms with unfinished walls and no stick of furniture. They spent a sleepless night, as rats looked out through holes. But they had come to stay. The next day they bought furniture, and Mrs. Andrew Muhl brought them a meal.

The local priest apologized when he returned from his circuit ride. Previous to their departure, the sisters had heard that there was an epidemic in Waco, and had wired ahead to ask if they should come. The layman who received the message in the priest's absence certainly didn't want to scare them away, so had simply said, "Come on!"—and had forgotten to give the priest the message that they were coming.

Once there, they must have experienced serious culture shock. Lockport had been at least a little like Belgium. In inviting the sisters to Lockport, Bishop Timon (writes Sister Mary Louise), after explaining that in Lockport "there were two churches: one, for the English-speaking; the other, for the Germans; the French went to either," had said, "'It seems that the holy Providence of God is sending you to us at the moment when the people greatly desire the establishment of a convent and school in Lockport.'"[9] Texas would be different!

One week after their arrival, the sisters announced the opening of school. There was no school building—but at first there were no students either! We have no record of how the enterprise was advertised; perhaps it was announced at the High Mass on Sunday. In New York, various ethnic groups, mostly Catholic, would have clamored for a school of their own. Texas was different! We know from the community diary that a week later only eight people other than the sisters attended the Sunday Mass. We have conflicting records of that first school day. Classes were to be held in the church, so it is likely that registration was there. The diary says that no one came, but Tom Bloomer, a resident of Sherman for fifty years, insisted later that he had been there. He reported that the sisters let him go home early.

On October 2 an Episcopalian family registered, and one Catholic student came. Ten pupils were registered by October 6. The story of that beginning is summarized by Sister Mary Louise:

> Mother Emilie, already discouraged at the poor prospects, was planning to return to Lockport; then yellow fever broke out in the neighboring settlements. No butter, no eggs, no meat, no vegetables could

9. Corcoran, *Seal of Simplicity*, 82.

be procured in Waco, which had been quarantined against the menacing disease. Then Sister Mary Angela became critically ill with dengue fever; she was confined to bed for weeks. In the meantime, Mother Emilie herself became a victim for a short period. When she saw her plans to leave thwarted at every turn, she decided that God wanted her to found a house. When the quarantine was lifted, instead of taking her Sisters home, she wrote to Lockport for two more.[10]

Mother Emilie's resolve was not for the long term. "Do not buy property," she instructed, intending to withdraw at the end of the school year. By that time, the pastor was well pleased with what was happening in his small community, and urged the sisters to stay; but uncertainty remained.

Would it be wise to stay? A letter draft written by Mother Emilie reveals her anxiety.[11] Addressing an unidentified recipient, she desperately speaks "with an open heart to expose the perplexity" in which she finds herself. "In Belgium," she says, "the Jesuits had been advisors to the Sisters," had, in fact, given them their "religious spirit and religious existence." She yearns for such guidance in the present situation. The tone of the letter, the reference to a previous conversation in Chicago, and the emphasis

10. Ibid., 202.
11. SSMN archives, Fort Worth.

on the Institute's relation to the Society of Jesus suggest that the addressee is a Jesuit spiritual director. The total submission of judgment seems to echo Saint Ignatius' famous letter on obedience, especially when it is placed in contrast to the challenging tone of her subsequent letter to Bishop Dubuis. She explains her dilemma:

> The information we received from the Bishop, the priests of Waco, and other persons, does not correspond to the reality we find there. To our great disappointment, we learned upon our arrival that there are in Waco only twenty-five Catholic families, with six school-age children.... More heavily populated areas offered us by the Bishop have been given to other Sisters. There is also the threat of yellow fever, the danger of which still exists in the months to come.... The small number of people, and hence the limited amount of good to be accomplished, seem not to balance the risk of the life of the Sisters. And finally, the absence of Catholic families would seem to offer little hope of vocations to the Institute.[12]

Her question is clear: "Should we establish ourselves in Texas or not?" Assuring the recipient of her fervent prayers for the guidance of the Holy Spirit,

---

12. Actually, in the years that followed, more than twenty women entered the Congregation through the Waco foundation. (Personnel lists, Sacred Heart Academy; SSMN archives, Fort Worth.)

she states: "I will receive your response as an oracle from heaven, and whatever the difficulties I will follow it."

If indeed a final draft of the letter was sent, and Mother Emilie received the response as "an oracle from heaven," the answer must have been yes, since not only did the sisters stay, but they were authorized to begin building.

There remained an interim of uncertainty pending Bishop Dubuis' clear confirmation. Mother Emilie's letter to him dated January 24, 1874, reveals her anxiety:

> Monseigneur,
>
> Permit me to address a few lines to your Lordship on behalf of our Sisters in Waco.
>
> A year ago Madame/Mr. John Murphy spent six weeks in Lockport and had an opportunity of becoming thoroughly acquainted with the aims and spirit of our Institute.
>
> Finding, as they saw, that nothing could be better in Texas or suit the wants of Texas better, they tried to persuade us to an undertaking of which we never dreamed, the more so as we were convinced the Superior General would not permit it. Well, M. Murphy saw your Lordship and wrote to us in the most glorious terms of all you had said, and I received at the same time from your Lordship, through your V.G. [Vicar General], an invitation to 5 or 6 places with

the kind promise to offer us all you could. (The letters I still preserve.)

We availed ourselves of this promise to obtain permission from the S. General, who in considering establishing a province (5 or 6 places in your diocese) left us free to act.

Meanwhile I received another letter from your Lordship, stating your return to Europe & authorizing us to correspond on the subject with your V.G. and finally with the Rev. L. Bussant.

A year's consideration seemed to us not too long a time for so important an undertaking, but Rev. L. Bussant did not seem disposed to wait, as his last letter begged to be informed by telegram whether we could not be there by the middle of [date illegible]. If not, he would provide for his school by taking secular teachers.

As we had gone so far and were now sure of your Lordship's good feelings toward us, we thought it better to go at the cost of any sacrifice. Our Sisters left immediately, full of zeal and good will, assuming all the expenses, which was not a little undertaking for a young community like ours. I accompanied the Sisters, hoping to have the honor of a personal acquaintance with your Lordship, but after six months of misery had to return without this favor, my duties calling me home.

When we arrived in Texas, Fr. Bussant charged himself with informing your V.G. of our arrival, and when your Lordship returned from Europe, the Sisters were told that they would soon have the honor of a visit of your Lordship having to travel in that direction.

Now the Sisters inform me that you have passed twice near Waco in the act of installing . . . a new community in Dallas, but that they had not been favored by a visit. Of course, Monseigneur, I must infer from this, or rather, what must I infer, I know not. I fear F. Bussant is not on the best terms with your Lordship. If such be the case, it is to be regretted that we were directed to him. I do not see what fault can be imputed to us which would thus turn all your kindness into indifference.

Now, Monseigneur, if nothing can be done for our Sisters, in the name of God they must come back. In Europe as well as here it will be a subject of astonishment, for I have not made a mystery of my transaction with you, Monseigneur, and your respected clergy, but have consulted . . . , following the advice of several Bishops and Distinguished Priests, who will sympathize with us, for they know the sacrifices we have made for this little mission.

If our Sisters have to come back, will our little community in Lockport alone be charged with all the expenses? Indeed, I cannot for a moment suppose that Monseigneur would permit us to be dealt with so unjustly, but on the contrary, I like to think that in the end it is only a trial and that your Lordship will be a father to those Sisters who so cheerfully made every sacrifice, hoping to do a little good in Texas under your paternal protection.

Pardon the unusual length of this letter and the freedom with which I have stated matters to you, Monseigneur. I considered it necessary to do so.

Hoping to receive soon a favorable reply, I have the honor to remain

Sister Emilie[13]

The letter is informative, especially as regards the influence of the Murphys on the Waco foundation, and the importance of the venture to the communities in Lockport and in Belgium. The importance of ecclesial approbation is also clear, but we may find our sympathies with the bishop when we read the note attached to the letter:

Last Saturday after having travelled nearly two thousand miles, I arrived here, where to relieve me, I found this letter, to which I answered this morning, on the 27th, from Dallas. I wrote to Rev. Bussant telling him

13. Original in Catholic Archives of Texas, Austin, TX. A copy is in the SSMN archives in Fort Worth.

that I was wishing to pay my visit as soon as possible. I did not receive any answer from Rev. Bussant in these 20 days, I could not go uncertain to meet him.

      Pray for yours in Christ,

         Dubuis[14]

  Meanwhile, life had gone on. Noteworthy events are recorded in the diary: moving to the new building, first Mass in the convent chapel, permission to maintain the presence of the Blessed Sacrament. Each new student's name is treasured. By the second of November there are twenty-six pupils! Priests come to visit and are served a meal. Dr. Brown looks in on Sister Mary Angela, who is slow in recovering from dengue fever.

  On March 9, 1874, the diary announces a great day: Bishop Dubuis visits, bringing with him Father P. F. Chandy, pastor of the parish in Corsicana, and Father Claude Marie Thion, responsible for the Sherman–Denison area. The bishop takes tea with the priests who accompany him.

  Obstacles were cleared, contracts were signed, and building began. On June 10, 1874, Sister Mary Angela bought property on Eighth and Washington. The title would be held by the trustees of Lockport. The bishop donated two lots, and the sisters bought a third with money loaned by John Murphy. He charged 12-percent interest, never mentioning that

14. Ibid.

he was borrowing the money at 16 percent. Where, we may wonder, did they expect to get money to pay?

Undoubtedly the community was always in debt. Struggling to make mortgage payments, the sisters lived as simply as possible, and when the final mortgage payment was made, they used that house as equity for the next foundation in the area, thus acquiring another debt.

But that question was secondary. The emphasis was on life. On July 5, six children made their first Holy Communion. Waco had never witnessed such an event! Baptismal vows were renewed and the children made an act of consecration to the Blessed Mother. God's word was being planted, and God's love witnessed! It was for this that the sisters had come.

On July 15 of 1874, the first brick was laid for the new building, the one we knew as Sacred Heart Academy. Young sisters made three-year vows, and a house was opened in Corsicana. Sisters Stephanie Hoolie, Rosalie [surname unknown], and Mary of the Crucifix Defour were assigned to that house, but there were frequent visitors from Waco, even exchanges of personnel between communities.

Monthly retreats were regularly held on such subjects as obedience, fidelity, mortification, charity, modesty; yes, and death. Those were the challenges of their daily lives; there must have been moments of weakness, but they got through them, and the work went on.

4

Unlikely Spread

WE WHO know the busy schedules and crowded classrooms of later years may wonder why the sisters stayed, and how they spent their time. Diaries suggest that they were struggling to survive. Sister Stanislaus Eagan, diagnosed with muscular rheumatism, was visited by doctors on several occasions. She had been one of the first American-born girls to enter the Congregation, and must have been in her early or mid twenties. Sister Angela was still not strong. Dengue fever tends to leave an aftermath of weakness. The school certainly enjoyed a flexible curriculum as students were added one by one. Had they been to other schools? Elementary education was not yet mandated. Had the children been homeschooled? Were some starting at the very beginning of formal study? Surely there was a close personal relationship between each child and tutor. The program must have been systematic, since the first graduates—Mary Mills, Eva Silvers, J. Johnson, and J. Lyons—received their diplomas at the Opera House, on June 28, 1881.

How did the sisters manage? Certainly at least one of them cooked; besides the sisters and two boarders, the diaries report that there were frequent guests. On March 9 Bishop Dubuis came, and with him were Fathers Chandy and Thion. "They stayed for breakfast," the diary reports several times, and "they stayed for tea." Too discreetly for our taste, the diary says that the bishop "made some arrangement about the building of a school." We know that he bought two plots of land.

We may suppose that more than food was involved in those clerical visits, since Father Chandy was pastor of the parish in Corsicana, while Father Thion was responsible for the area of Denison–Sherman. Both, we know, requested and received Sisters of St. Mary for their parishes. It would seem that Waco was to become a hub for Catholic education in North Central Texas.

The diary entry for July 6 suggests what powered the sisters' dedication. "The children made their First Communion. There were six 1st Communicants. It was the first time such a ceremony took place in Waco"—and, we might suppose, the first such ceremony in all of Central Texas. "In the evening they renewed their Baptismal vows and made the act of consecration to the Blessed Virgin." Surely it was for this that the young community had left family and friends, had come to an area that knew few human comforts and even fewer securities: that children might come to know and love the Lord, and to be sustained by the sacraments he offered them.

Sister Mary Angela went to the diocesan center in Galveston on June 8 "to make some arrangement for a building" in Waco, and on Friday, June 12, 1874, Feast of the Sacred Heart of Jesus, Sister Mary Angela bought a third plot of land on Washington Street, adjacent to the property of the bishop. It was the "Trustees of St. Joseph Academy, Lockport" who took responsibility for the purchase. On the same day, the contract was signed for the building of the school, an action rooted in faith, hope, and love, and having little to do with human certainty. The Waco diary reports that the first brick was laid on July 15; and thus was triggered what Sister St. Patrick McConville refers to as the launching of the school building program of the Sisters of St. Mary in Texas, a program whose achievements spanned over forty years:

> Sacred Heart Academy, Waco, 1873
> Our Lady of the Sacred Heart Academy, Corsicana, 1874
> St. Francis Xavier Academy, Denison, 1876
> St. Joseph Academy, Sherman, 1877
> St. Ignatius Academy, Fort Worth, 1885
> Our Lady of Good Counsel Academy, Dallas, 1902

> Academy of Mary Immaculate, Wichita Falls, 1905
> Holy Name School, Fort Worth, 1909
> Our Lady of Victory College and Academy, Fort Worth, 1910
> St. Edward School, Dallas, 1912[1]

At the completion of her list, Sister St. Patrick remarks: "With the exception of the meager funds the good Bishops were able to give them, the Sisters of St. Mary erected all these schools at their own expense."

In his address at the Golden Jubilee celebration of St. Mary's Church of the Assumption (1923), Bishop C. E. Byrne paid tribute to that effort:

> There is a linking-up, then, between the foundation of these Sisters, with the heroic missionaries of Texas in the early days, and the heroic missionaries of Missouri and the Northwest, the pace that gave Galveston and this part of Texas its first great missionaries.... Only twenty-four years before the coming of the Sisters of St. Mary, this city had been surveyed, and only twenty-three years before their coming to this city, it received its charter, set up its own government, and ruled itself as a city of this state; so that when there is talk of pioneers in Waco, the Sisters of St. Mary cannot be left out of the question, for their lives have

---

1. McConville, "A Brief History," 40.

been devoted to the establishment of God's kingdom on earth, and their influence has been so great and their history is so worthy and deserving that they must always be regarded as among the pioneer settlers of Waco.[2]

Impressed though we might be by the eloquence of Bishop Byrne, we may be more touched by the stories of the sisters who established the tradition of which he spoke. In the Waco diary we read of the first four sisters' struggle in Texas.

Sister Mary Angela, whom we met as Jennie Healy, had been born in England of Irish parents and educated in Belgium. A member of the second group of Sisters of St. Mary to come to America, she would spend most of her life in Waco. She was the sister of Mary Margaret Healy, who had married John Murphy; it was that couple who initiated the invitation to Waco. But who were Sister Adolphine and the two young sisters who, we read, renewed temporary vows?

Sister Adolphine Dalton entered the novitiate in Lockport in 1872 and came to Texas the following year. The date of her perpetual vows is uncertain, but we know that she spent the rest of her life in Texas. Hers was the first death at Our Lady of Victory (1913), so she is buried in Fort Worth. Sister Stanislaus Eagan entered the novitiate in Lockport

2. Ibid., 54.

in 1866. We know that she eventually returned to Lockport and was buried there in 1902. Sister Patricia Dwyer, on the other hand, who had entered in 1869, must have lived out the whole of her consecrated life in Texas, since she was buried in Wichita Falls, in 1921.

As we have noted, the first enterprise those sisters undertook was called Sacred Heart Academy—a title that might hold our attention for its academic as well as its religious implications. It set a precedent to be followed by most of the schools established by the sisters, eight of which were called "Academy." In our day that title is reserved to such sophisticated groups as the American Academy of Arts and Sciences. The word is actually derived from the name of the place where Plato and his followers held their philosophical discourses. Milton, in his *Tractate on Education*, written in 1644, uses the word to denote a school in which "a complete and generous education" is given. How might such a term apply to a school that enrolled sixteen children of various backgrounds in a frontier town of Central Texas? In her unpublished manuscript, Sister St. Patrick explores this subject, saying:

> Three types of institutions for secondary education have developed in the United States: the Latin grammar school, emphasizing classical learning for the aristocracy

and those preparing for the professions; the academy, stressing more practical subjects for the better-to-do middle classes; and the public high school, throwing open to the masses secondary education of both classical and practical courses.[3]

The culture represented by the academy, she explains, "was broader though less concentrated than the Latin grammar school, and it especially stimulated a greater expansion of subject matter." While emphasizing the broad cultural influence of offering secondary education for girls and providing dormitories for students whose homes were at a distance, Sister remarks that the academies were vital for training teachers for rural areas.

Such institutions were especially important in the post-Civil War era, when the funds set aside by previous legislators for education had been canceled out by more urgent needs, such as the building of railroad connections; consequently, during the period of Reconstruction almost all the schools were private ones. Although the Texas Constitution of 1869 stipulated free public schools, a state superintendent, and compulsory attendance, very little was accomplished, and when in 1873 the old Southern democracy was returned to power, the people reverted to private schools such as had existed before

---

3. McConville, "A Brief History," 59.

the war—schools that were available only to the affluent.

The situation offered options to the young community as it established policies. They might have established safe enclaves for Catholic children, protecting them from the very Protestant environment. But from the beginning, Protestant parents asked admission for their children, and the sisters were doubtless pleased to fill out the student body with children of other families who were struggling to maintain Christian values. True to the spirituality of the time, they also treasured the possibility of conversions. There were a few secret baptisms when it was thought that children were in danger of death. Though records say that Protestant parents demanded assurance that their children would not be proselytized, the clearly Catholic identity of the sisters and their devotion to both God and the children brought about a number of requests for baptism—sometimes of whole families.

A favorite story is that of a mother who demanded of the sisters assurance that her little girl would never be allowed "to say Mass." The assurance was freely given, but we are told that not only the child but even the mother eventually requested baptism—and that two of her sons became Jesuit priests! Perhaps it was such experiences that gave the sisters the courage to continue through the hot summers and the lean winters of their Texas experience.

As for economic policy, it was clear from the beginning that the sisters' concern was the Christian education of children. The policy was simple and inflexible: no Catholic child was to be turned away for lack of funds. The diaries frequently express concern for meeting mortgage payments, and even grocery bills. A letter written a few years later laments that "fewer than half the children can pay, and only two of the boarders." It was the need of the child, not of the sisters, that was the deciding factor.

Even more surprising than the survival of the Waco enterprise was its rapid expansion. Certainly a number of facts contributed to that success. The population of the South was scattered, since the fertile Black Lands of Texas lured immigrants from the Deep South, where the plantation-centered culture had fallen to the Civil War. Boarding schools rendered a real service to families for whom transportation was a major problem. Roads existed, but early letters speak of ox-drawn wagons, cattle drives, and mud that made even walking a perilous enterprise. But the sisters went bravely on to establish academies.

Sister St. Patrick speaks of "four different conceptions of education" prevalent at the time. "Whereas a majority saw [education] as the private concern of the parents," she reports, "others saw it as an evangelizing agency, forming Christian character." As for the public schools, some saw these as the right of all, while one tradition held that public education was by right a service only for paupers. The academies staffed by the sisters brought together pauper and aristocrat, with neither teacher nor fellow students much aware of which was which.

There were ecclesial reasons too for the success of the schools. The councils held by American bishops in Baltimore had recognized that the American public schools offered an environment clearly hostile to Catholics. The Bible was a basic text of education, but only the King James Version was allowed. Requests to allow Catholic children to bring their own Bibles were consistently refused. The assumptions of Protestant teachers colored their teaching, which roused the resentment of Catholic parents. For this reason, the bishops mandated a Catholic school in every parish—an order that sent pastors scurrying to find sisters who would teach. It was assumed that they would also build the schools!

Among those pastors were Father Chandy, of the Immaculate Conception parish of Corsicana, and Father Thion, of the Denison–Sherman area. Having accompanied Bishop Dubuis on his first visit to the Waco establishment, they were quick to ask for Sisters of St. Mary for their own communities. Developments within and outside the Congregation enabled the sisters to respond positively.

One was the growth of membership in the Institute. In spite of the troubled state of the country immediately after the Civil War, twenty-two young women had entered the Lockport novitiate between 1864 and 1873. The vast area of Central Texas, with its rapidly growing immigrant population, corresponded with the Congregation's eagerness to evangelize; but the small community was far from the motherhouse in Lockport.

Even from the beginning, Mother Emilie had spoken of the need for clusters of communities in Texas. Small groups should not be isolated, but would enjoy exchanges and mutual support. The development of the railroad made this possible.

Corsicana, fifty-six miles north of Waco, was the first step toward this development. Sister Mary of St. Joseph, Sister Adolphine, and Sister Stephanie Hoolie left Lockport, New York, at 11:30 a.m. on Tuesday, August 25, and on Saturday, August 29, at 2:00 a.m., they arrived in Denison, where they were met by Father Vitalus Quinon, the local priest of Denison, and Father Claude Marie Thion, of Sherman. After changing cars, they arrived at Corsicana at 9:30 the same morning. Sister Mary Angela, superior of the Waco community, was at the station to meet them. More fortunate than some of their predecessors, they found a little house that was scrubbed and furnished. Enthusiasm was high as the school opened on September 7, with five girls and six boys. On September 8, 1874, the *Denison Daily News* said of Our Lady of the Sacred Heart Academy:

> The Sisters of St. Mary have opened a boarding and day school at Corsicana under very favorable auspices. The course of study comprises all the branches of a thorough English education, and with the personal care and attention of the Sisters, the school will, no doubt, gain steadily in popularity. Corsicana is located in a healthy section of the State, and the charges for board and tuition are placed at the lowest possible figures.[4]

The lowest figure was actually zero, since the policy there, as in all St. Mary schools, was that no Catholic child was to be refused because of inability to pay. By October 2 the sisters were preparing children for First Communion, and on October 8 there was a reception for the bishop.

But on Tuesday, November 17, the boast of the "healthy section of the State" was put to the test. Sister Stephanie Hoolie complained of fatigue. Various remedies were tried. On the twenty-first, Dr. Watkins diagnosed typhus. The diary gives reports daily: "The fever continues. . . . There is inflammation of the brain. . . . Father Chandy administers Extreme Unction. . . . Viaticum. . . . Father Chandy

---

4. Quoted by McConville; "A Brief History, 41.

recites prayers for the dying." On November 30, the diary reports simply that "Sister Stephanie died at 7:30 this evening." That short sentence marks the end of a very short life.

Katie Hoolie had been born in Lewisburg, Pennsylvania, on September 11, 1853, and had entered the novitiate in June of 1872. She celebrated her twenty-first birthday in Corsicana, and two months later was interred in the convent garden there. "A little cross was erected above the grave, and it was enclosed next day with a fence."

To Mother Emilie, who with such enthusiasm had sent forth the little missionary band, this death must have been a shock, no less than to the two sisters who survived in Corsicana, and to the small community in Waco. No word is recorded of the grief of the parents, who could not attend their daughter's funeral. Since the telephone had not yet been invented, there was not even the comfort of a familiar voice to communicate the news.

But life went on. The following school year opened on September 4, 1876, "with nine girls and ten boys. Five of the girls are new, and there is one new boy. There is one Catholic girl among them, and only four of the boys are Catholic."

Perhaps it was the small percentage of Catholics in the student population; perhaps it was a kind of indifference on the part of the Catholic community. Whatever the cause, on September 17 the bishop announced to the people that he was withdrawing the sisters from the Corsicana school to send them to Sherman, where they were "both wanted and needed." Sister Mary of St. Joseph went to look at property in Sherman. In November she went to Lockport for community consultation, which must have been favorable to Texas, since she returned on January 1 bringing with her Sister Aloysia Corcoran. On January 13, 1877, authorization came from Lockport: "Commence Sherman at once." No time was wasted; on January 15, 1877, Sister Mary of St. Joseph Cary and Sister Claire Markley boarded the train for Sherman.

But between the Corsicana and the Sherman foundations, there was another one. We first hear of it in a letter from Sister Camille Clara to a "Mr. Kemen," probably the father of Mother Emilie, written in January of 1876:

> About two years ago, Sister Superior went to Texas to found a new house. In a certain place named Denison, where she passed, she saw only tents with sign-boards: "Washing is done here." "Bleaching is done here." It all looked like an immense fair. On her return, three months later, most of the tents had disappeared and were replaced by comfortable houses. Today it is a flourishing city with a population of about 10,000,

and we hope, with the help of God, to establish a house there.[5]

"The climate of Texas is delightful," she reports, "much like the south of France. Now, in the month of January, the peach trees are in bloom, and soon there will be fresh vegetables." (Clearly this was a midwinter letter. One may wonder what she wrote in August!)

The same writer, given somewhat to superlatives, reports that the Waco school is well established and "the Sisters of St. Mary have acquired the reputation of being the best teachers in Texas . . . and have the children of the best Protestant families in their school. . . . Some of the more advanced students have even come to the boarding school in Lockport, so that there is hope of the Texas institutions being feeder schools for New York." Picturesque details are added:

> In Texas, civilization is not as advanced as in the north. Most of the wagons are drawn by oxen, and sometimes there are fourteen harnessed to the same vehicle. At the head of this procession is a man on horseback who, like an army general, goes constantly from one side to the other to stimulate his horned soldiers. According to Sister Superior, it is very comical. There are also

---

5. "Life of Mother Emilie," 89. See also Corcoran, *Seal of Simplicity*, 203–4.

in Texas immense prairies where cows and oxen browse at leisure; if you can catch one, it is yours. Consequently, meat is very cheap here: 5 cents a pound.

Much was new and exciting, but bridges, especially those of language, were not easily crossed. The Corsicana diary was written in French, with an occasional English word thrown in. We learn, for example, that "un serpent a tué une chicken!" A skunk, too, was killed in the backyard. A decidedly Texan experience!

But something else was happening in Texas. The trains that had brought the sisters south were changing the way business was done, and the small community from Lockport was caught up in the enthusiasm of the time. Though stability was hard to maintain in a fluctuating society, a support system quickly developed among these small communities.

Spared the expense of travel (railroad passes seem to have been readily available to them), the sisters enjoyed regular interchange among the communities. We read that young teachers went to neighboring convents for help with music, both vocal and instrumental, as well as for assistance in teaching algebra and geometry. It might be said that a nascent province was already present.

The Corsicana foundation seems to have fluctuated the most. Opened in 1874, it was threatened with closure by the bishop in September of 1876.

He would send the sisters to Sherman, where they were "both wanted and needed." They did go to Sherman—but remained for a time in Corsicana too. By April 1, Our Lady of the Sacred Heart Academy in Corsicana reported the loss of many students as public schools expanded; fewer than twenty children remained in the Catholic school; but by March of 1879 the decision was made to build, and the cornerstone was laid on August 31. By September of 1982, we know from the diary, almost all the day students had gone over to the public school. The sisters apparently withdrew; but in January of 1885, sisters went from Waco to reopen the Corsicana school. Closed in 1887 (perhaps just for the summer), it reopened in August of that year with twenty-six pupils, of whom most were boarders. The diary lapses, but there must have been another growth period, since on March 5, 1898, "nineteen of our boarders" attended a cultural event at the local Opera House.

The neighboring parish in Ennis (St. John Nepomucene, founded in 1904) presented new challenges to the sisters. It was expected that at least some of the classes would be offered "in Bohemian." The priest helped arrange for a young woman who spoke both Czech and English to help sisters and pupils. When it was realized, however, that the sisters were expected not only to supply her with room and board but also to pay her $30 a month, the arrangement was canceled. We have no record of how the problem was resolved.

Though the sisters came to be much appreciated in the Corsicana school, an important element was lacking: the diary often reports that there was no Mass. Sometimes we are told that the pastor was absent; at other times no reason is given. Occasionally a priest passing through celebrated the Holy Sacrifice in the chapel or the church. When the Sister Assistant to Mother Teresa Brennan, the General Superior, visited the southern houses in 1906, she reported the decision that the houses of both Corsicana and Ennis were to be closed for lack of spiritual support of the sisters. A sense of loss is reported among all the small communities of the area.

But other foundations had occurred. Establishments in Sherman and Denison brought the community to North Texas. The diaries of those schools record new experiences. In a letter from Denison dated December 22, 1875, Father Francis Derue, the local pastor, writes to Mother Emilie in Lockport, urging the community to purchase "the house and property of our banker, Mr. Perry," for $4,600. There is urgency in his request. "I am waiting for the approval of the Bishop. The public school will close next month. It is the best opportunity to start a school in Denison." His postscript adds new urgency: "Please answer *immediately*."

We understand that request when we realize that the compulsory-education law required only four months a year of attendance. Classes begun in January could be finished in May.

The sisters' response could hardly have been more prompt. The first entry in the Denison diary is dated January 24, 1876, when four Sisters of St. Mary arrived in Denison from Lockport "for the purpose of opening a school in the former residence of Mr. Ed Perry, which they had purchased." (In an entry for January of 1878, we read that the sisters have spent two hours trying to help Mr. Perry understand that his property was sold at too high a price and is not suited to their purposes.)

Sister Augustine Barry, one of the original pioneers in the American venture, came to Denison with Sister Adolphine Dalton, Sister Anne Donohue, and Sister Benedictine Burns, all of whom had made their novitiate in Lockport. When Sister Anastasia, Mother Emilie's younger sister, joined them in 1878, the school was already flourishing, the classes filled with one hundred day students and sixteen boarders.

Early diaries report no major crises. The arrival and departure of each boarder is faithfully recorded. As superior of the Denison community and chairman of the board in Sherman, Sister Anastasia seems to shuttle between the two places at least once a week. Already in April of 1879 the foundation of the new building is begun, and in June of 1879 the sisters move to their new home. The neighboring convents seem to "twin," much as Waco and Corsicana had done. Each community visits the other for such special events as the awarding of prizes, but in general, visits seem frequent and casual.

Life, however, was not without difficulties. The priest who had been so eager for the sisters' coming proved to be unstable. Diaries record sisters' requests to Father Thomas Hennessey to use his influence with that pastor to get him to offer Mass regularly. "It is not possible to adhere to the school schedule when the sisters have not yet had breakfast at 8:00 a.m." In December, a serious situation occurred when he began to spend hours a day at the convent, talking irrationally, so that the sisters finally had to call in Mr. Perry, who "dragged" him from the house. Two policemen escorted him to Galveston. Father Joseph Blum came to offer Midnight Mass for the parish, but otherwise there was no Mass in the pastor's absence. He returned in mid-January. The diary reports that the sisters sent his meals to his house for a time. Eventually he returned to the convent for breakfast, for dinner, and occasionally for supper. Visiting priests, of course, joined him for meals. There is no record of compensation for this service.

Death struck a girl in the sisters' care. Isabella Hall, "a little Indian child," left the boarding school to go to a cousin's house, apparently because of illness. After a short time, a messenger arrived at the convent to announce that the child was dying. The sisters hurried to her side but found her already dead. Priest and doctor also came too late. Baptized the previous year, the child had been confirmed three weeks earlier. She was buried from the Catholic church. Her mother was unable to come till a few days afterward, and the sisters had the sad duty of accompanying her to the grave.

In October of 1881, Sister Johanna Welsh became critically ill. She died on November 7. Sisters and pupils walked to the cemetery. (Sister Magdalen Sullivan, who had died in Sherman on July 10, 1880, was already buried there.) But the life of the community seemed to flourish, as did the life of the city, and the school was to continue well into the twentieth century.

The story of Denison and Sherman cannot be told without reference to the arrival of trains. At the beginning of his book *Katy's Baby: The Story of Denison, Texas*, Jack Maguire explains that Denison "was conceived and developed by the Katy Railroad as its southern terminal." The first Katy engine pulled into Denison on Christmas Eve, 1872, and when the Houston Texas Central Railroad "met the Katy there in 1873, their joining connected the U.S. by rail for the first time." Maguire refers to Sherman as "a bustling but raucous frontier town," and quotes an unidentified author as saying that "it had no citizens, but its saloons and dance halls were peopled with 'denizens.'"[6]

Sherman, however, had been organized in 1846, and was a thriving town when the sisters arrived, at the request of Bishop Dubuis, in 1877. The town, ten miles south of Denison, had been incorporated in 1857. Though clearly a frontier town, it boasted a Catholic community that had just completed the erection of St. Mary's Church, in which Bishop Dubuis had already confirmed thirteen people.

The story of St. Joseph Academy begins with Bishop Dubuis' initial invitation to the sisters, issued on September 17, 1876. His remark that the sisters were "wanted and needed" in Sherman evidently made quite an impression, since the diary tells us that it was only "a few days later" that Sister Mary of St. Joseph went to Sherman to look for suitable property! The telegram Mother Emilie sent four months later said, "Commence Sherman at once"; and at once it was begun.

January 15, 1877, found Sister Mary of St. Joseph and Sister Claire on the train to Sherman. At their late-night arrival they were met by the pastor, Father Louis Granger, and by the faithful Father Hennessey, who on many occasions proved a strong friend to the sisters. The two priests brought them to the home of Mrs. Mary Craycroft, with whom they

---

6. Maguire, *Katy's Baby*, 1.

spent a few days while they tried to procure furnishings for their small house. The community was fluid during the first days: on January 17, Sister Josephine Harrahan and "Miss Mack" arrived, and on January 19 Sister Mary of St. Joseph returned to Corsicana. During the months that followed, she went from Corsicana to Sherman every Saturday morning and returned to Corsicana every Thursday evening. Just before school opened in September, Sister Maria McShea, Sister Aloysia Corcoran, and Sister Agnes Connolly were added to the personnel of St. Joseph Academy. The role of Miss Mack is not made clear in available sources. She is identified only as a "companion" to Sister Josephine. Might she have been something of an "associate" a century before we had formal associates? It is clear that laywomen played essential roles in each of our foundations.

When school opened in September 1877, the student body was made up of thirty-eight girls and four boys. In the following January, Mother Emilie appointed Sister Emma Fitch as the first superior of St. Joseph Academy. Records indicate that she was a dynamic person whose vision was not limited by existing structures. More classrooms were needed; girls from remote areas would need dormitory facilities. By 1881, plans were in place for a new brick building that would include two large classrooms, which could be converted into a hall for school programs. There would be a refectory, a chapel, a dormitory to accommodate eighteen boarders. The attic, which was not completely finished until December 26, 1889, would be used as a dormitory for the sisters, and a linen room. The dynamism of the enterprise is recorded in diary entries:

> Sept. 5, 1881: Today the house in which we live is being moved in order to make room for the new building.
>
> Sept. 8, 1881: The old house is moved and the foundation for the new one is commenced.
>
> Oct. 1, 1881: Mass in our chapel said for the success of the new building. After Mass, Father Blum blessed the new foundation.
>
> Dec. 13, 1881: A letter from Lockport containing money for our new building.
>
> Apr. 10, 1882: Easter Monday. No school because we are moving into the new building.

Sister St. Patrick captures the sense of life and growth:

> On May 12, 1882, a board of eight trustees was named for St. Joseph Academy, and Sister Emma was appointed President of the Board. At a meeting of the trustees on that day, it was agreed that the property on Travis Street, bought from Mr. B. Fairchild in 1876, should be used for the

teachers' residence, and also that the house on Walnut Street, bought from Mr. P. F. Goben in 1879, should be used for schools: one house for the little girls, and the other for the little boys. It was further decided that the building in construction on Travis Street should be occupied by senior pupils and boarders.[7]

Busy as it was, the project in North Texas did not stand alone. Sister Mary Angela, who was in charge of Sacred Heart Academy in Waco, was appointed to the board of St. Joseph Academy in 1882. Significant of community bonding is the fact that she invited her new associates there to come to Waco for the laying of the cornerstone of the new addition to the school in July of 1882.

Expansion in Sherman went on. As the student body and the boarding school grew, we read that Sister Emma went to Denison to "buy the property of Mr. and Mrs. Crooks." We read nothing of lawyers or real estate agents. Sister Emma had entered the Lockport novitiate in 1869, probably as a very young woman, but, like Sister Mary Angela and other early leaders, she simply did what had to be done. The house on the property she bought furnished additional dormitory space and room for the art department. One of the outside buildings was used for a laundry, and a bake oven was built there.

---

7. McConville, "A Brief History," 60.

Meanwhile, a curriculum was being developed. Archives preserve the daily schedule for the first division of the First Class in 1880:

Morning

    8:30 Bell rings for school.
          Morning Prayer
          Catechism of Christian Doctrine (for Catholics)

    N.B. Every Monday morning the first Period is devoted to a "Civility Lesson." (It stresses conduct and the observance of the rules of the school.)

    9:00 Mathematics
    9:30 Etymology
    10:00 Science
    10:30 Calisthenics in the Playroom. (Dumb-bells are used, and students learn to March.)
    10:50 Study Period
    11:15 Grammar
    11:55 Angelus rings for dinner period. (Many pupils go home for dinner.)

Afternoon

    1:30 School is called.
    1:35 Penmanship
    2:00 History
    2:30 Literature
    3:00 Mythology
    3:30 Memory Gems
    3:50 Evening Prayers

4:00 Dismissal[8]

The work of organizing, building, and supervising while maintaining the structures and practice of religious life took its toll on Sister Emma's health. On August 19, 1884, just as the sisters completed preparations to receive those coming to the annual retreat, Sister Emma suffered a massive heart attack and died. Grief-stricken, the community closed ranks and moved on.

But there were other deaths: in Sherman, Sister Margaret Mary Crosby died a year after Sister Stanislaus; in Denison, Sister Barbara Garrett had died a week before Sister Emma, and a week later, Sister Loyola Beatie, who had returned north with Mother Emilie, died in Lockport.

The cost in money of these early foundations is beyond comprehension; the cost in energy, in health, in life itself strikes us with awe. Clearly everything is gift, is response to the great Gift of God's own Son. And gifts are shared. Looking at the early history of the Sisters of St. Mary, we realize that each foundation is a separate enterprise, but that each is a part of something larger. Intersecting board membership, exchanges of personnel, money sent from Lockport, all point to a shared persona. Active participation of Sister Mary of St. Joseph, member of the original missionary band, and of Sister Anastasia, member of the second band and

---

8. Ibid., 62.

sister of Mother Emilie, made clear the union with Belgium. The pronoun "we" had rich meaning for our founders; it has rich meaning for each of us who find our identity not only in the present moment, but in all that has gone before and all that follows.

Sacred Heart Academy
Waco, Texas
1873–1946

Our Lady of the Sacred Heart Academy
Corsicana, Texas
1874–1908

St. Xavier Academy
Denison, Texas
1876–1968

St. Joseph Academy
Sherman, Texas
1877–1968

St. Ignatius Academy
Fort Worth, Texas
1885–1961

Our Lady of Good Counsel Academy
Dallas, Texas
1902–1961

Our Lady of the Rosary Academy
Ennis, Texas
1904–1907

Academy of Mary Immaculate
Wichita Falls, Texas
1905–1966

Our Lady of Victory Academy
Fort Worth, Texas
1910–1961

St. Edward Academy
Dallas, Texas
1912–1968

Mother Emilie Kemen
First Superior of the Sisters of St. Mary
in America

Community of Sisters of St. Mary
St. Xavier Academy
Denison, Texas, 1903

Margaret Mary Healy Murphy and husband, John Bernard Murphy

5

"Hell's Half Acre"

THE LATE nineteenth century was a period of rapid change. The Sherman diary reports that in 1890 not only did the MKT Railroad come into their city, but electric cars replaced mule-drawn vehicles on city streets, and that in 1894 electric lights were put into the classrooms.

Fort Worth was somewhat later in developing, since Caddos, Wacos, and Indians of other tribes still dotted the surrounding prairie when John Peter Smith, the ink hardly dry on his diploma in Ancient Languages and Mathematics, opened the first school in the city in 1854. He "found the task uncongenial," remarks Oliver Knight, but promoted consciousness of the need for education. Even in 1856, Fort Worth was "on the ragged edge of uncertainty," still thought of as a frontier village, and Birdville was the seat of justice for Tarrant County.[1]

---

1. Oliver Knight, *Fort Worth: Outpost on the Trinity*, 33.

But in 1873, a boon was announced: the railroad was coming! The State of Texas offered large land grants if the Texas & Pacific Railroad would reach Fort Worth by January 1, 1874. Other investors were assured of large grants for their businesses under the same condition. But as the long-anticipated celebratory banquet was in progress, word came that Jay Cooke & Company, one of the world's most potent financial centers, had failed. The nation was thrown into panic. Since people had borrowed money on the presumption that the railroad would inflate the value of both land and commerce, an economic slump devastated the area.

The state legislature postponed the deadline for arrival of the train, but when postponements were no longer possible, the whole town turned out to complete the line. Knight tells the fascinating story of the desperate means employed to build makeshift tracks across the Sycamore Creek.[2] Finally the train rolled into town on July 19, 1876. In the course of this activity, Knight tells us, "Fort Worth had erupted into the wildest town in western Texas," its population including, besides courageous entrepreneurs, "cowboys, professional gunmen, swaggering buffalo hunters, squint-eyed gamblers, and saucy dance-hall girls."[3]

2. Ibid., 74–75.
3. Ibid., 77.

The town grew rapidly. The courthouse was built at the north end, and was soon surrounded by several well-developed businesses, a few churches, and some rather elegant homes. This area, known as "uptown," was in contrast to the south end of Main Street, which had come to be known as "Hell's Half Acre." It was in this area that the Galveston Diocese bought land for a church, and it was to this section that, in 1885, Father Jean Marie Guyot joined Bishop Nicholas Gallagher in inviting the Sisters of St. Mary.

It hardly seemed an appropriate neighborhood for a convent. Stagecoach robbers and train robbers made their center there. Knight tells us that it was "a human cesspool that resisted efforts of law enforcement agencies for years"—in part because of some businessmen who saw the cowboys and their friends as an excellent source of income, not to be discouraged by "too much stringent enforcement of the law closing all places of amusement that attract them."[4] Presumably neither stringent laws nor the nearness of church, priest, and nuns brought undue restriction, since James Talmadge Moore tells us that it was only in the 1890s that "footpads, harlots, holdup men, gunmen and their ilk" were replaced by homemakers.[5]

---

4. Ibid., 73.
5. Moore, *Through Fire and Flood*, 173.

But even earlier, the south end of town was home to many hardworking families. Railroad workers, largely Irish immigrants moving down from Chicago after the Great Fire, made their home in the area. They were so numerous that when the parish voted on the name to be inscribed on the cornerstone of its new church in 1888, its former patron, Saint Stanislaus, lost out to Saint Patrick.

Once again, the community served by the sisters was largely immigrant, and because displaced people cling desperately to those who share their language and their customs, there were distinctive groups. In a delightful letter published in the May 9, 1975, edition of the *Fort Worth News-Tribune*, Madeline Williams recounts a story of her mother's youth.

The French pastor, Father Guyot, who had come to Fort Worth in 1884, dreamed of building "a little Chartres" in this West Texas town, but money was hard to come by. Perhaps a popularity contest among the girls would bring in some money! Innocently, he invited Madeline's mother, whose parents had come from Germany, and Katie Baker, of Irish descent, to enter the contest. That pitted a fräulein against a colleen and aroused ethnic rivalries that were painful to all. But it helped pay for the building, whose cornerstone, laid in 1888, was truly built by immigrants.

The Fort Worth community faced another problem. The Diocese of Galveston, to which Fort Worth belonged, had experienced a period of difficulty. The much-loved Bishop Dubuis, exhausted and ill, went to Europe. Bishop Pierre Dufal, the former vicar apostolic of Eastern Bengal in India, was appointed coadjutor bishop with the right of succession. Bishop Dubuis gave him power of attorney to transact business during his absence. Though his experience would have led him to respond to situations somewhat differently from the ways already established, Dufal hesitated to make changes, knowing that Dubuis might return. Frustrated, he soon offered his resignation, which was accepted by the Holy See in January of 1880. Dubuis returned briefly, and appointed Father Theodore Buffard as chief authority in the spiritual affairs of the diocese; as chancellor, the person to be responsible for finances, he named Father Louis Chaland. He then went to Rome and officially resigned the administration of his diocese—but retained his title. Further disturbances raised questions about authority in the diocese.

It was a difficult situation that the newly appointed Bishop Gallagher faced when he arrived at his diocese in 1882. The papal decrees had made it clear that he was to be elevated to the rank of bishop, but that Dubuis, in retirement in France, was to retain the title of "Bishop of Galveston." The extent of the difficulties, rivalries, and general disorder in the diocese is reflected in Bishop John Quinlan's advice to Gallagher to "accept like a man" the appointment he was offered.[6]

The Fort Worth parish experienced repercussions of the problem. Bishop Gallagher, as administrator of the Diocese of Galveston, wrote to Mother Emilie in August of 1884. In urging the sisters to take charge of the parish school in Fort Worth, he informed her that "a community of four religious," headed by someone called Mother Theresa, was in Fort Worth. These religious claimed, he said, "to conduct an academy also."[7] Is this the same as the "St. Stanislaus School" for which a diocesan record reports forty-eight scholars in 1884? Since they had come without episcopal invitation and were without canonical status, the bishop thought it necessary to get other teachers for the parish school. Mother Theresa and her group refused the bishop's request to leave.

Sister St. Patrick's narrative reports that those sisters were liked by the people, a fact which caused parishioners to be slow in accepting the new community of Sisters of St. Mary. We find no record of

---

6. Ibid.

7. From Mercy Hospital of Loredo, in a letter to Miss Beniti V. McElwee, we learn that a Mother Theresa Muldoon, whose relation to the official Congregation of Mercy Sisters was tenuous, acted on her own initiative in coming from Galveston to Fort Worth and establishing "St. Joseph Academy," probably in 1882. A copy of the letter is in the SSMN archives in Fort Worth.

how the problem was resolved. Did the two groups teach at different sites? An early chart indicates a small school on the northwest corner of the church property. Perhaps Mother Theresa's group continued to teach there. We know only that the classes of the St. Mary's day school were first taught in the church, where the sanctuary was curtained off each day after Mass. The school, however, grew and flourished, becoming St. Ignatius Academy.

Despite the challenges, on September 3, 1885, Sister Anastasia Kemen, superior of St. Xavier Academy in Denison, accompanied Sisters Claire Markley and Patricia Dwyer to the new site. They were joined a few days later by Sister Adolphine Dalton, Sister Camille Clara, and Miss Mollie Kirby to complete the faculty. This was no provisional arrangement. Two small houses were purchased: the residence of Jacob Smith, to be used for classes, and an adjacent building owned by Charles Roche, to be used as a residence by the teachers. The diary reports that the number of students enrolled in September 1885—twenty-nine—multiplied rapidly, so that 1888 saw the commissioning of the four-story limestone structure that in our day is recognized as a landmark.

The faculty must have expanded too, because we read that in October of 1886, Sister Elizabeth Lynch became ill and nine days later died. Having entered the community in 1876, she had probably pronounced perpetual vows the summer before she was sent to Fort Worth. Small wonder Mother Emilie expressed concern for the health of the sisters!

But we read of a greater tragedy, the death of a child. Discreet as always, the diary says only that "an accident" happened to Lillie Bennett. Sister St. Patrick, probably depending on oral tradition, tells the story in more detail. The child, a day student, came in from the cold and rushed to the stove for warmth. When her clothes caught fire, she dashed out in panic and, before anyone could reach her, was severely burned. Her mother was called, as well as a doctor. A bed was prepared in the parlor, and the sisters watched with her during three weeks of suffering. According to Sister St. Patrick's source, the child had asked to become Catholic, but the mother had refused. The sisters baptized her the night before she died; and the grieving mother asked for baptism a year later.[8]

In spite of the difficulties, the sisters found their place in the local community. Besides weekday classes, they taught catechism on Sundays and attended "both Masses," Benediction, and often a sermon in the afternoon. They visited the elderly and the critically ill, and exchanged visits with the Sisters of St. Mary from the Waco, Sherman, and Denison communities.

---

8. McConville, "A Brief History," 75.

Other bonds were formed as well. St. Joseph Hospital had been founded in 1883 as a railroad hospital, and the Sisters of Charity of the Incarnate Word formed treasured friendships with the Sisters of St. Mary. Visits to and from the hospital are recorded regularly, and the diaries state that when the superior of the hospital died, the St. Mary sisters kept the night watch with the corpse. When death visited the community at the school, the "hospital Sisters" were a priceless support.

The diary does not record the difficulties of the growing city. We know, however, that in 1886 the Knights of Labor, one of the oldest labor unions, confronted Jay Gould's stranglehold on the railroads. Not only did men refuse to work, but women and children sat on the tracks to prevent the trains from moving. In April of 1886 a gunfight ensued at Buttermilk Junction, near 2200 South Main. Jim Courtright, a former city marshal and at this time head of his own detective agency, was the best known of the gunmen; a journalist later to be known as O. Henry reported incidents. And the sisters went on teaching, preparing the children for a changing world.

The new world was already present. In less than twenty years the school found itself in the business district of a rapidly growing city, and recognized as a significant center of education. The sisters realized that expansion was urgently needed. The boarding school, they reasoned, would be better served if it was nearer the outskirts of town; and they saw that relocation as a major project. (The story of Our Lady of Victory will be found in a later chapter.) Meanwhile, they would construct a large but less expensive building just southeast of the original structure of St. Ignatius to accommodate their own growing population.

But something new was happening. Across the tracks were growing neighborhoods. How could the sisters reach out to the children of those families? A cottage on the corner of Kentucky Avenue and Hattie Street was bought to be used as a school. In 1906, forty-five children "below sixth grade" registered in what became known as St. Ignatius Annex. Much later, when Holy Name Church was built, the sisters moved the school to that site, where it became identified with the parish.

Susan Pritchett, longtime archivist for Tarrant County, was not able to find a demographic description of South Fort Worth for 1906, but remarked that it was probably the families of railroad workers who lived there. "St Ignatius was well situated and well established at that time," she added, "and would be meeting the requirements of a wealthier population, so the sisters reached out to a newer need."

Once more we find the pattern identified in the introduction of this document:

> An effort meets with success. (St. Ignatius is thriving.)

> But someone in the group notices a new need (young families of the working poor) and calls it to the attention of the community.
>
> The Congregation makes a decision: without neglecting the current project, they will respond to the new call.

Such a decision marks a moment of crisis. Those who have struggled to bring the current work to fruition might reject the new idea, leaving it unmet or sending the visionary off to seek her own solution.

The decision for St. Ignatius Annex was a landmark, crossing a new frontier. It would not mean buying the house next door or building an addition to an existing structure. This change would require that sisters leave the convent each morning to take public transportation to a new area. It was a pattern that would be followed often in the years ahead, when in Fort Worth alone, sisters would go out each day to the parochial schools of Holy Name, San José, and St. Mary. In Waco, Sister Mathilda Laufkotter and companion would go each day to St. Francis Mission; in Wichita Falls, sisters would likewise go to the mission parish of Our Lady of Guadalupe. Decades later it would be a simple matter for sisters who serve different parishes to set out each day from the same convent. Apostolate and community life would find ways, not only to coexist but to be mutually supportive.

The initial decision was made after careful thought. Sister St. Patrick tells us that Sister St. Leo Boylan, who was in charge of St. Ignatius, was directed by Mother Teresa to purchase a house to be used as a school. We are told also that the work was encouraged by both Bishop Edward Joseph Dunne of Dallas and Father Guyot. It was a simple beginning. Only those who, in all sorts of weather, waited patiently (or impatiently) for the streetcar or bus, or who tramped the hot streets of Waco to the river area of the Mission, truly know the cost of the decision. Those whose faith and human development were born or nourished in these "outposts" know its value.

6

Beyond the Cluster

EVEN BEFORE the first Sisters of St. Mary came to the United States, Mother Claire, always concerned for the spiritual support of her sisters, had expressed the hope that they might establish themselves in Buffalo, the diocesan center of Eastern New York; but Bishop Timon had reported that the needs of that Catholic community were already being met. Consequently, it was only in 1887 that the Sisters of St. Mary established Annunciation Convent, their first house in the heart of the diocese. Something similar occurred in the southern area of the American experience.

Sister St. Patrick mentions that as early as 1873 Bishop Dubuis had "intimated that he would like the Sisters of St. Mary to found a school at Dallas," but she notes that "it was not until after the second division of the diocese that a formal invitation was extended to the Sisters of St. Mary to open a school in the episcopal city of the Diocese of Dallas."[1] Situated in the newly established Blessed Sacrament Parish, the school was to be called Our Lady of Good Counsel Academy [LGC]. The opening days follow a familiar pattern:

> Sisters from earlier foundations are involved.
> Beginnings are simple, often marked by hardships.
> Laypersons of the area, especially women, play a significant role in the life of the community.

Diary entries give details:

> Sunday, Aug. 17, 1902: Sister Mary Angela and Sister Helena [McShea], Superiors of Waco and Sherman, came down to Oak Cliff to inspect the house and to order a few of the most necessary articles of furniture so that they would be in readiness when the other Sisters would arrive.
>
> When Sister Superior [Sister Isabel] and Sister Bonaventure arrived in Dallas, they were met at the station by Mrs. Tierney with her carriage.[2]

On Monday, August 18, they were taken to their empty house, which had been rented from a Colonel Bettarton. Located on Eleventh Street at

---

[1]. McConville, "A Brief History," 79.

[2]. Diary, Our Lady of Good Counsel Academy, Dallas, Texas; SSMN archives, Fort Worth.

Pecan Drive, it consisted of six rooms, a bathroom, and a very small storeroom. Their furnishings consisted of four cups and saucers donated by Sister Mary Bernard Reilly, Superior of Denison. They had brought no food. A lunch (which they served on a box!) was donated by a man in a restaurant.

As the furniture had not arrived, they were forced to borrow chairs for two of the sisters; a box was found for the third, while the fourth was obliged to stand. About five o'clock that evening the house furniture was delivered; but the kitchen utensils did not come until half past eight, so the sisters were without supper. The furniture was placed as soon as possible, and the sisters spent their first night in Oak Cliff.

> Aug. 19: Sister Mary Angela and Sister Helena called on Rt. Rev. Bishop Dunne. Sister Superior and another Sister from the Orphanage called this morning before Sister Mary Angela returned home.
>
> Aug. 20: Statue of the Holy Family, from Sisters of St. Vincent. [St. Paul Hospital had been established in 1896.]
>
> Aug. 26: Two large fires not far from the convent.
>
> Aug. 27: Another large fire, still larger than those of yesterday.

The austerity of life is clear in diary entries, but it is always mentioned in the context of the donor's generosity and the gratitude of recipients.

> Aug. 30: This has been a red-letter day. The old gentleman who sawed our wood donated us four peaches and made a reduction of 75 cents, which we greatly appreciated. Shortly after, the postman came, bringing a "Welcome Song" from Lockport and a letter from Corsicana telling us the Sisters had sent us a bag of coffee, which again put us in high spirits.
>
> Aug. 31: Today the coffee arrived!
>
> Sept. 3: Another red-letter day. The morning mail brought us a letter from Sister Mary Angela, Superior of Waco, containing a check for twenty dollars, which is no small amount in our poor purse. In the same mail, a letter from Sister Louise, Superior of Ft. Worth, containing ten dollars and thirty cents worth of stamps.[3]

Clearly, money was being spent, but generally in direct service of the apostolate:

> Sept. 2: Piano arrived from Fort Worth. It was selected by Sister Louise and Sister Mary of the Incarnation. The make of the piano was a Behr.

---

3. Ibid.

> Sept. 20: Sister Superior went to Fort Worth this morning, . . . rented a piano for the school, and transacted other business.
>
> Oct. 9: About twelve o'clock at night we received from Mother Teresa a message which read, "Purchase Villa Rette."
>
> Oct. 24: The desks ordered from Mr. Bryan in August arrived at last!
>
> Oct. 25: Sister Superior of Denison, Sister Superior of Sherman, Sister Superior of Corsicana, Sister Aloysia, Sister Gabriel, and Sister Cecilia came today to be present at the dedication of the new Sacred Heart Cathedral tomorrow.
>
> Nov. 18: Torrents of rain. Sisters caught in storm after Mass. Consequently without breakfast, and as rain continued, could neither send for nor get any dinner. At last, Mr. McGinn kindly went down to 10th Street in all of the rain, and having seen but one of us, brought back under his overcoat a lunch for one, which was immediately devoured, and as two children had arrived in the meantime, a few lessons were heard, after which we returned home more dead than alive.

We understand their situation when we remember that they were still living in the house on Eleventh Street—a distance of four blocks of unpaved passage from the church. It was only on

December 13, 1902, that they would move into the "villa" that later generations knew as Our Lady of Good Counsel Academy.

Clearly there are moments when the community laughed together. The diary writer tells another story:

> Jan. 16, 1903: While we were enjoying our evening recreation we were suddenly startled by a loud knock at the front door and rapid walking up and down the front porch, which extends halfway around the house. Sister Bonaventure, of renowned bravery, at once started out to investigate, but after going down two steps and not receiving any answer to her anxious inquiry of "Who's there?" her terror increased at the continued pacing of the yet unknown visitor, and concluding that by some means or other, he had gained admittance to the house, she returned with lightning rapidity to hide behind her chair. As soon as she had succeeded in concealing herself, a well-known voice cried out, "No Mass tomorrow!"

But among the stories that speak of struggle, of youthful inexperience, even näiveté, we find a strand of business acumen. Another entry, seemingly for the same date, reports: "The deed of Villa Rette arrived, but was found to be improperly executed, and was returned to Alabama for correction.

On the arrival of the deed, the notary had gone to his eternal reward. Hence, another delay."

Rev. William Hoover, in his book *St. Patrick's: The Story of 100 Years*, offers an observation about the Sisters of St. Mary, whom he had known as a student, as a pastor, and as a business associate: "The sisters seemed imbued with fierce determination to succeed, to build something of worth and endurance. Clear thinking, deliberate goals, an uncanny familiarity with finance, and steady confidence are among the impressions from their records."[4]

Paying the bills, however, was a constant challenge. Music lessons were always important, financially as well as culturally (five of the first twenty-eight students took music classes), and we recognize the bishop's cooperation in that effort when we read that on June 7, the pupils of Sister Mary of the Incarnation "gave a musical hour for Bishop Dunne, Father Hayes, and Father Maginn." On the other hand, when in 1904 the sisters requested permission to receive boarders, the bishop replied that he could not consent to that "without breaking my word." They might, he suggested, sponsor five or six entertainments as a way of raising money—a suggestion that would cause any teacher to shudder! The one effort the sisters made in response to it is reported as having delighted the audience, but it was a financial failure.

---

4. Hoover, *St. Patrick's*, 66.

We may assume that the refusal of permission to open the school to boarders was a result of an agreement with the Ursuline sisters, who since 1874 had conducted an excellent academy and boarding school for girls in Dallas. The archives contain a fragment of a letter, written presumably to Mother Teresa, in which Sister Helena reports that she has received a phone call from the bishop concerning an advertisement stating that Our Lady of Good Counsel was established "for the education of females," and that the statement in the charter had to be amended for fear that "the Ursulines will say we are coming into their territory." A partial solution to the problem was reached in 1905, when the Sisters of St. Mary were allowed to accept as boarders students who were following a business curriculum, which was not offered at Ursuline. Taught by Sister Aloysia, the business classes were popular, and the boarding school became successful.

Housing was not, however, without problems. While they lived in the convent at Eleventh and Pecan, the sisters walked four blocks to the school, a two-story building that housed the church and two rooms for the priest on the second floor, and classrooms on the first. In 1930 that building was condemned, and restructured into a one-story church. It was relocated at the far end of the block on which Villa Rette was located, on land donated by the

Sisters of St. Mary. The Villa, beautiful though it was, was in constant need of repair.

Meanwhile, something new was in the making. The Sisters of St. Mary had applied to the Holy See for pontifical recognition of the Institute. To receive it, they needed to make some changes in their form of government. A general superior could hold office for no more than two consecutive six-year terms, and a local superior could not remain in office for more than six consecutive years.

The first news appears in the diary on November 10, 1906. In a letter sent from Lockport, Mother Teresa gives explanations and directions relating to the first Local Chapter, which is to be held in Fort Worth on November 17. That "strictly confidential" letter, dated October 16, 1906, explains that, for our Constitutions to be approved in Rome, and our status to become pontifical rather than diocesan,

> ... our system of government and our economical system must be transformed. We must have a General Chapter at which the General Superior and the general Officers will be elected. ... The General Superioress may only be elected for six years, or at most, for twelve years.
>
> There must be two provinces: the Belgian province and the American province, each of which shall be governed by a Provincial Superioress appointed for three

> years, and the local Superioresses must also be changed every three years. Furthermore:
>
>> We must have a general Treasury to provide for the needs of the Institute, a provincial Treasury for the needs of each province, and each house must give part of its income to the provincial Treasury.

We can imagine the excitement as the sisters came to realize the implications of these changes. Sister Mary Angela, for example, had been superior of the Waco house since its founding in 1873, and handled many of the business concerns for other houses. The financial arrangement meant that instead of borrowing money from one another, each community would contribute to a central fund to which all could apply.

The diary reflects these matters only impersonally. The first provincial chapter would be held at St. Ignatius.

> Nov. 17: Sister Raphael went to town to get passes over the T. and P. to Fort Worth. Mr. Everman gave them cheerfully. The morning mail brought passes for six Sisters over the Interurban.
>
> Dec. 14: Sister Superior very busy preparing for her trip North to the Provincial Chapter. Sr. Pauline is to go as Delegate.

For the most part, life simply went on as usual.

> May 31 [1907]: Rev. Father Hayes made an address in which he said that it is admitted by Bishop and clergy that the Sisters of St. Mary are the best teachers in the state.

One may wonder on what research this statement was based, but it must have been encouraging to the young community; definitely something to write home about!

> Dec. 1: Sister Bonaventure, Sisters Emily and Bridget went to Holy Trinity College for Solemn Benediction and Vespers.

That mention of Holy Trinity College may be a point of contact with a little-known correspondence between Mother Teresa, Superior of the American Province of the Sisters of St. Mary, and Vincentian Father Patrick Finney, President of Holy Trinity College, Dallas, Texas. The college was situated in what would become known as the Turtle Creek area of Dallas, on the plot later occupied by Jesuit High School.

A.M.D.G.   St. Joseph's Academy
Lockport, October 13, 1908

Rev. Patrick A. Finney, C.M.
Holy Trinity College
Dallas, Texas

Dear Rev. Father,

Kindly accept our grateful thanks for the interest you have taken in our community in Texas. I am constantly hearing of some new act of zeal and devotedness on your part, Reverend Father, and your letter of the 6th . . . is again a proof for which I feel deeply indebted.

If the time for the first fifty thousand dollars worth of improvements on this land could be prolonged to five years, we could perhaps see our way to it, and get the sanction of our Reverend Mother General and her council. We have but just received the permission for the Fort Worth Academy. We have, however, sent copies of your letter and that of Mr. Rather, and while awaiting their answers, I have asked Sister Margaret Mary to do all she can to get the time prolonged. I would not like to take less than twenty-five acres, for although it may be years before our Texas houses be formed into a separate Province, we would then find it difficult to procure a large enough tract in so desirable a location. I will be in Texas about the middle of December, and I hope to have the pleasure of meeting you then, Reverend Father. If the offer could be held open until that time, I would be very thankful. I feel sure, Reverend Father, you will use your influence to this effect with these gentlemen. Assuring you again, Reverend Father, of our deepest gratitude,

> and of our united prayer for the success of your zealous works, and begging a remembrance for our Community at the Holy Altar, I am very respectfully ...
>
> Mother M. Teresa[5]

The letter to which Mother Teresa refers is perhaps the following. Undated, it is in the folder with her letter to him.

> Dear Mother,
>
> I take this opportunity to offer you my sincere and grateful thanks for the kind remembrance you sent me at the close of your retreat. Kindly offer my thanks to the Sister who wrought the beautiful things you sent me. Though it is rather late to be offering you my thanks, nevertheless I can assure you that they are none the less sincere.
>
> Sincerely hoping that you and all the members of your community are enjoying the blessing of health, I remain in the love of our Lord and his Most Holy Mother
>
> Very sincerely,
> Patrick A. Finney, C.M.[6]

Further correspondence indicates that Father Finney, speaking to the manager of the property, tried to negotiate a donation of twenty-five acres of

---

5. SSMN archives, Fort Worth.
6. Ibid.

land the owner had bought at $225 per acre. He was offered a compromise: a donation of ten acres and special pricing for the rest.

The same folder includes information about other available land in the Dallas area. It would be thirteen years before Texas would become a province, and certainly property in that area would by then have become unavailable as well as cost-prohibitive. We can barely imagine the daring that it took to consider paying $50,000 over a five-year period. The arrangement was never concluded; but it did happen that Holy Trinity College changed its name to "The University of Dallas" before it closed its doors, and that the Sisters of St. Mary were able to obtain that charter for their own foundation in Irving, and to educate their novices there in the middle of the century. The long-range planning and the financial acuity referred to by Father Hoover (see above) are evident here.

All that was still in the future, but spirits were high. The LGC diary for 1911 reports:

> July 12: Twenty-two of the Sisters left here at 7:30 a.m. to go to the Cathedral to be present at the ceremony of Consecration. . . . At 2:30 p.m. the Sisters from the Cathedral returned. . . .

A week later there was another celebration;

> July 19: The great event of dedicating the Academy of Our Lady of Victory takes

place today. All the members of our little community are there except four.

Nor was that the last of special occasions:

> July 25: Mother Albertine and the heads of the different Academies in Texas, also some few of the Sisters, left here at 5:30 a.m. to attend Mass at St. Edward's Church, East Dallas. After Mass the Right Reverend Bishop broke the ground for the new school which is to be erected this year. Rev. Mother and each of the Superiors in turn removed a spadeful of earth. Rev. Mother Albertine, Sr. Julia, and Sr. Mary Theresa left for Denison. Sr. Superior of St. Ignatius Academy and of Our Lady of Victory Academy left for Fort Worth.

On July 30 Bishop Dunne celebrated his first Pontifical Mass. A plenary indulgence was granted to those who assisted at it and complied with the usual conditions. The Church in the diocese was growing, and St. Mary was sharing that growth.

7

And Farther North

WHEN, IN 1903, Father J. Groessens invited Mother Teresa Brennan, the Provincial Superior of the Sisters of St. Mary in America, to send sisters to Wichita Falls to establish a school, he could make a very tempting offer. As pastor of Henrietta, of which Wichita Falls was a mission, he recognized the rapid development going on in the area. The wheat fields of Oklahoma and of the Texas Panhandle were ripe for harvesting, and Frank Kell, a staunchly Catholic parishioner, had built mills; the Fort Worth and Denver rail line was available for transport; and Joseph Kemp had assured the city a permanent water supply by building Lake Wichita. Voted the county seat of Wichita County, the town boasted two banks, telephone and telegraph service as well as electricity, and a local newspaper. The people's recognition of the importance of education was evident not only in the existence of an elementary school and a high school, but also in the popularity of such organizations as the Unity Club, a Study Club, a Shakespeare class, a musicians' club, and an elegant Opera House.

There were thirty Catholic families, Father Groessens reported, and they wanted a Catholic school. The sisters might expect 100 to 150 day students and a good number of boarders. The city would give ground valued at $25,000—that money to be gathered from the businessmen of the city—and he himself would offer $1,000 toward the building of the school, and also donate benches and other school furniture. Mother Teresa's response was not available to Sister Barbara Kelly, whose thesis is the source of most of the above information, but it is evident that the response was positive.[1]

Adding to the sisters' welcome, Mayor Anderson Bean wrote Mother Teresa assuring her of the pleasure of the citizens in learning of the promised foundation. With her typical business acumen, Mother Teresa asked the mayor to get the block surveyed and staked under the legal title of "the Sisters of St. Mary, St. Joseph's Academy and Industrial Female School of Lockport, New York."

The land was given, but erecting as well as staffing the school would be the responsibility of the sisters. In a letter to Mayor Bean, Mother Teresa assures him that "our best endeavors will be exerted in

---

1. Kelly, "Academy of Mary Immaculate," 64.

giving the good people of Wichita Falls an institution of learning of which they may be proud."² Her promise was fulfilled, as memories and pictures of the building confirm.

Sister Mary Bernard Reilly, the superior of St. Xavier Academy, was named to oversee the construction, since she had already performed that service for the Denison establishment. She and Sister Johanna Hermon made frequent trips to the site, and enjoyed the hospitality of the Hund family, whose home was across the street from the new building. A well-loved oral tradition tells the story of Sister Mary Bernard discovering, on one of her visits, that the brick being used was not in conformity with the contract. Immediately she walked, brick in hand, to the bank that held the contract, and asked to see the president. He confirmed her finding, and the error was corrected.

The school opened in September of 1905, and the charter is dated March 8, 1907. School registers list boarding-school students from the North Plains of Texas and from Oklahoma, Kansas, Missouri, Colorado, and New Mexico. Many were not Catholics, but their parents were pleased with the education offered by the Academy. Besides the religion classes offered for Catholic students, requirements for graduation from the high school included the following:

2. Ibid., 17.

> four years of English: grammar, composition, literature, rhetoric;
>
> mathematics, three years: algebra I and II, and geometry, plane and solid;
>
> social studies: ancient, medieval, modern, English and American history, and civics;
>
> languages: Latin, Spanish, French;
>
> science: physical geography, biology, physics, chemistry, zoology, botany, and astronomy.[3]

Typewriting, stenography, and bookkeeping were given as electives. Elocution and calisthenics received particular attention.[4] Given this curriculum, which was typical of all the academies, it is hardly surprising that graduates from the program were considered competent to serve as elementary-school teachers.

The school opened on September 5, 1905, with a Mass celebrated by Bishop Dunne in the convent chapel. Boys were accepted in grades 1–8; girls were welcomed also as boarders and as high-school students. Minutes of the meetings of trustees (all Sisters of St. Mary, listed under their legal names), 1906–1958, report consistently that "the schools are flourishing." Two areas of concern that receive less glowing reports are "improvements needed" and

---

3. Ibid., 22.
4. Ibid.

the state of the debt: a room would be partitioned into music rooms; a galvanized fence would be built at a cost of $1,100; a servants' house would be built, and a cold storage added to the kitchen; block 260 would be bought for $4,500, for which payment money would be borrowed from the City National Bank, and other loans and notes accepted.

In February, $2,000 was borrowed from a Mr. Cartwright to help repay the City National Bank, the First National Bank, and the Denison Bank. Each month some personal notes were redeemed. In 1910 "an urgent demand from St. Ignatius Academy made it obligatory to borrow $3,000 from the City National Bank at Wichita Falls." By December this amount was paid back to the City National Bank, through the kindness of the "Provincial *Econome*, Lockport, N.Y."

And on it goes: "We owe the Denison Bank $7,700 @ 6%, and the Waco Convent $600 interest-free." In March of 1911, "our indebtedness to the Provincial House and the Lockport Bank amounts to $55,362.80," but "to the Denison Bank our debt is decreased by $6,498." In some months, there is no reduction to principal, though interest is faithfully paid. But woodwork must be painted, an infirmary room added, the science room moved and updated. The city demands that sidewalk be laid on Ninth Street, at the expense of the sisters, at an estimated cost of $10,000. Still other improvements continue to be found necessary. Debts notwithstanding, "the schools are in flourishing condition."

The principal source of income, Sister Barbara points out, is the student body.[5] "Terms per Month" are listed as follows:

Board	$30.00
Tuition according to Grade	
First and Second Grades	3.00
Third and Fourth Grades	3.50
Fifth and Sixth Grades	4.00
Seventh and Eighth Grades	4.50
Academic Department	5.00
Laundry Charges	1.50
Piano Lessons and Use of Piano	8.00
Violin Lessons	8.00
Voice (Individual Lessons)	8.00
Voice (In Class)	[No charge]
Expression (Individual Lessons)	10.00
Entrance Fee (Only on First Admission)	5.00
Library Fee (Annual)	2.00
Laboratory Fee (Annual)	5.00
Graduation Fee	20.00

---

5. Ibid., 38.

The date of the bulletin from which this information is derived is not noted, but the breakdown of charges is typical of the era. Simple arithmetic suggests the impossibility of paying debts of more than $85,000 on this income.

But the people of Wichita Falls were known for their generosity. Not only were there cash donations, large and small, but there were personal gifts as well: a cow, another cow (and her calf), a horse, and much-needed services. It is reported that when wood was needed for the furnace, Sister Superior would call together John Oechsner, Charles Wolf, Henry Hund, and Charles Parker, and promise that she would ask Sister Johanna to make a cherry pie for them if they would chop some wood. Years later, they reported that the pie was delicious!

Besides implementing various economies, the sisters sold Block 260 at a value that had considerably appreciated. However, it would happen only in February of 1947 that the Secretary could announce, "The house is now out of debt!"

The diaries of the Academy of Mary Immaculate frequently report severe storms. Especially notable is the one that disrupted the Odd Fellows picnic at Lake Wichita on April 21, 1928. "Practically all Wichita Falls was there," Sister Barbara reports, and school children were delighted to receive free tickets. It was, however, to be remembered as "the most terrific electrical storm in thirty years." Picnickers were drenched, and the last of them arrived home at about 8:00 p.m.

Recognizing the damage that such storms could do, the trustees of AMI commissioned the building of a storm cellar. Only once are we told that it was used—on May 8, 1909. Just as the boarders were preparing to retire, they were shepherded into the cellar. In late evening the storm subsided, and all returned to the convent, only to go once more to the cellar as the storm struck a second blow. The wind did extensive damage to the roof of the main building, and destroyed the shed used for the horses of the day pupils.

Whatever its difficulties, the Academy of Mary Immaculate certainly fulfilled Mother Teresa's promise to provide a school of which the city could be proud. Tangible proof of its educational excellence is offered in a listing of past and present leaders of the city. Its registers also indicate extensive service to the Church: besides the lay leaders of local parishes, the Academy also educated three men who would be ordained priests for the Diocese of Dallas–Fort Worth, and one for the Oblates of Mary Immaculate. Thirty-one graduates entered the Congregation of the Sisters of St. Mary, and three entered other religious communities.

When, in 1966, the building was vacated and eventually sold, the Congregation donated a substantial part of the price received to the diocesan

Notre Dame High School building fund. Several sisters continued to work in the new school, and even in the twenty-first century continue to play an active part in the life of the parish. Besides serving in the schools, several sisters shared in the Charismatic households. Thus laity, clergy, and religious continue to build up the Body of Christ in Wichita Falls.

8

A New Turn

THE LGC diary for 1912 speaks of the sisters' attending the ground-breaking ceremony for St. Edward's School. Subsequent entries indicate the close relationship the sisters in the new endeavor would enjoy with the established communities. We learn, for example, that on August 18, "the sisters [of LGC] resumed their daily visit to St. Edward's," and that on the nineteenth "Sister Raphael [O'Toole] and Sister Mercedes [Skiffington] went to Dallas, where they purchased furniture for the new school." We find visits in September from Sister Cecilia Byrnes and Sister Mary Teresa Lovell, "Sister Superior" Helena and "Sister Superior" Mary Bernard, and Sister Adolphine. Sisters Marcella Solan and Geraldine Larochelle arrived from the North, and Sister Mathilda returned from the North. The St. Edward's community went to LGC for Christmas dinner.

Though the visiting and interchange may seem to reflect what happens in every venture, this instance marks a new step in the Congregation's presence in Texas. Effectively, St. Edward's, though itself an academy, would open the door to the establishment of parochial schools. The land, contiguous to the church, was given the sisters by the newly consecrated Bishop Joseph P. Lynch, who had once been pastor there, and the school was the first in our province to be named for the parish in which it was established. Loans and contracts, however, bear the name of the provincial or local superior. St. Edward's introduces a new element of governance in its independence of the larger community across town, having its own faculty with living quarters on the second floor of the school building.

A clipping from a hectographed (purple ink) program proclaims its importance:

> On the twelfth day of November, 1911, at Dallas, Texas, the Corner Stone of St. Edward's School was blessed according to the ritual of the Roman Catholic Church by the Reverend Joseph P. Lynch, Bishop of Dallas, Texas, being the eighth year of the reign of our Sovereign Pontiff, Pius X; his Excellency, William Taft, [being] President of the United States; Honorable O. B. Colquitt, Governor of Texas; Honorable Stephen J. Hay, Mayor of Dallas; the Rev. J. H. MacRoberts, C.M., Rector of St. Edward's

> Church; Rev. Mother Felicity, Superior General of the Congregation of the Sisters of St. Mary; Rev. Mother Albertine, Provincial Superior of the American Province.

It was on August 31, 1912, that the local community arrived: Sisters Julia Macmaster, Rosario Murphy, Agatha Moran, and Francis Borgia. Sister Helena spent the first night with them and would return often as a guest. Sisters from other communities visited; Father MacRoberts urged the parishioners to drop by and get acquainted with the sisters, and even offered his help. Grace Hausen took the sisters for an auto ride, and the bishop, it is written, sent ice cream for dessert!

Finally, on September 10, school opened, with 105 pupils. (By September 16 there were 132.) The school was recognized as an academy, following the sisters' usual practice of offering elementary school to both boys and girls, but high school to girls only. It was unique in that no boarding school was attached.

The minutes of the trustees' meeting on August 12, 1911, define the purpose of the enterprise as "the education of youth and of young ladies, to confer degrees, grant diplomas, and to do and perform any and all necessary acts to carry into effect the said purpose of incorporation."

At the same meeting, the trustees voted to acquire a lot in addition to that given by Bishop

Lynch. Would not the business acumen noted by Father Hoover suggest that the Institute stop building until outstanding debts could be paid? But there is no record that the question was raised. Rather, there were children to be taught, the word of God to be spread.

We have few details of community life. Sister Rosario fell from a ladder and injured her wrist; on December 26, Sister Antonio was taken to St. Paul's Hospital for surgery, but she died on January 22. Mr. Sullivan came as janitor at $2.00 a week and board. He slept in the shed. Sister Geraldine died at St. Paul's on April 30. Typical Texas weather is reported, and there were numerous visits to and from other communities.

Even from the beginning, the high standard of education presaged the glowing reports to be received from the State Department of Education in later years: "some outstanding teaching in the grade school and in the high school"; "well-defined philosophy and practical subject offering"; "special praise for the teacher of Latin," and so forth. All this, though there were two grades in every class, and only two teachers assigned to the high school! The same record contains mention that several of the teachers had degrees from the Catholic University of America and others were working toward that goal. Clearly, priorities had been established for spending money.

So, like other schools owned by the sisters, St. Edward's always struggled with debt. The account books indicate that houses borrowed from one another and often had to borrow again to repay the money to a house in urgent need. The largest debt, however, was always to the Lockport bank, which usually offered a rate of interest slightly lower than average. Account books record a plea to be allowed to defer payment on another loan in order to pay a dentist bill. In 1921, the pastor requested that the Sodality prepare an entertainment for November 22, half the proceeds to go to the sisters! The sisters sent him a $10.00 check as a Christmas present, but "omitted the entertainment." Somewhat later, the local council decided to write a letter to the parents "who have been delinquent in paying their tuition" (April 9, 1922). But no child was told not to return.

In 1941 the loans were consolidated at a reduced rate of interest, so that some payment could be made on the principal. "It is understood," the letter states, "that any large donations received by any of our Schools or Convents will be used to redeem outstanding Bonds." Everything would be directed towards the children's education. The decisions, judged impractical by some, were, we may assume, based on the "simplicity of heart" that is the charism of the Sisters of St. Mary.

A New Turn   131

Our Lady of Victory Boarding School and
Academy, 1910–1961

9

A Home of Our Own

EARLY IN the history of Fort Worth, the town with its commercial enterprises and more elegant houses centered around the courthouse ("uptown"), leaving St. Stanislaus Church (later, St. Patrick's Cathedral) and St. Ignatius Academy in the unenviable area of "Hell's Half Acre." That situation would, however, shift with the arrival, in 1876, of the Texas & Pacific Railroad. Fort Worth would no longer be a mere stopping place on the Chisholm Trail; it would be a terminal, since cattle could now be forwarded by rail to markets north and east. The location of the terminal brought a swift and unexpected movement toward the south end of town, drawing the center of business as well as the cattle drive.

The railroad also caused a demographic shift, as many of its workers, largely Irish immigrants who migrated again from Chicago, found homes near both their employment center and the Catholic church. Even as the rapid expansion of both day school and boarding school of St. Ignatius Academy brought about the building of a large annex, the city saw the need to reroute traffic, so that the relatively new building had to be demolished. The Sisters of St. Mary recognized the need for a new location, with possibilities of wide expansion.

The land would need to be near the edge of town; but which edge? One proposal was to go towards Dallas, where the Interurban would connect the two cities. But research indicated that such a location would be less accessible to the people of Fort Worth. In addition, the large plot available was subject to flooding by the Trinity River. The sisters did their homework!

The other proposal was to move south, at the end of the bus line. That property was owned by a group of men, one of whom did not wish to sell. The first "Diary of Our Lady of Victory Academy," 1907–1922, reflects the lively community discussion of the question. Mother Teresa, Provincial Superior of the American Province, living in New York, realized that the decision needed to be made locally. She authorized Sister Helena, the superior at St. Ignatius, to choose a plot of not less than ten acres, for which "$15,000 might if necessary be paid." Months were spent in bargaining; meanwhile, Mr. Weatherford sold "the best part" of the proposed site, to the disappointment of the sisters.

Mr. William Shaw, who took an interest in the sisters' locating on Hemphill, advised putting the matter in the hands of a lawyer, Mr. E. C. Orrick, who recommended the purchase of the land owned by the four willing sellers, thus forcing Knight, the reluctant owner, to concede. A contract to purchase was drawn up. The eleven-acre parcel nearer the city, considered the more valuable, was to be purchased. However, "after carefully weighing the matter, and offering many fervent prayers to the Holy Ghost for light to make a judicious choice, the larger piece was taken. Later it was thought that it would be wise for the Sisters to own the entire twenty-six acres."[1]

Confident that the boarding school would flourish, the sisters purchased the other portion for $40,000, bringing the total cost to $55,000, toward which Mr. Mabery offered $1,000.

On March 25, 1909, ground was broken for the Academy. Rev. Robert M. Nolan, Rev. B. Diamond, and Rev. E. Park, CM, performed the ceremony, in the presence of Mother Teresa, Sister Helena, Sister Mary Bernard of St. Xavier Academy (the building expert), and many other sisters. Students came from St. Ignatius. Marshall R. Sanguinet drew up the plans, and a few days later, work began. A bank loan of $80,000 was signed by Mother Teresa, and secured by the mortgage of St. Ignatius Academy.

---

1. Our Lady of Victory Diary (1910–1922), 2; SSMN archives, Fort Worth.

On August 5, 1909, the cornerstone was laid, with the expectation that classes would begin on September 12, 1910. Not surprisingly, there were delays. Materials arrived late, plans were modified, and so forth. Clearly the building would not be ready: "The smell of fresh paint, the deafening noise of the hammer, and the general disorder which reigned throughout the building all seemed combined to prevent very much being accomplished."[2] But a date had been set, and friends advised that the date be honored, so the sisters, not unaccustomed to desperate situations, took the matter in hand.

> On September 9, eight Sisters left St. Ignatius Academy for "Our Lady of Victory Academy" on Hemphill.... Weaker hearts might have quailed at the stupendous task which lay before them, but was not Our Lady of Victory awaiting them at the portals to welcome, encourage, and give them strength and grace to accomplish all that Holy Obedience asked of them?"[3]

Their names march like troops across St. Mary history:

Sister Mary Bernard Reilly	Sister Mary Beatrix Furey
Sister Margaret Mary McShea	Sister Mary Stanislaus Connaughton
Sister Raphael O'Toole	Sister Mary Michael O'Rourke

2. Ibid., 3.
3. Ibid.

Sister Mary Esther McQuillen   Sister Mary Eugene Fox

All day they worked, stopping briefly to eat the lunch they had brought. They didn't even eat it all. Expecting to return to St. Ignatius for the night, they went back to work for the afternoon, and to their surprise, an announcement was made: "Supper will be served at 6:00." Nash Hardware had sent the range and set it up; the salmon, with bread and butter left from lunch, would be served, and—because Mr. Shaw provided cream—there could be a cup of Irish tea, proudly presented by Sister Raphael! The diary pays tribute to this "first cook at OLV," who overcame obstacles of poor wood and consequent smoke to make her presentation. The boxes of table linen and cutlery had not yet been opened, and the menu was limited, but the sisters rejoiced in being present at "the First Supper"![4]

Sustained by this luxury, they decided to spend the night in the new building. Sister Mary Julia and Sister Mary Patricia, who had also joined the group, decided to return to St. Ignatius, perhaps to hold down that fort, but the energized eight carried on. The city water had not been turned on, and the artesian well had not been completed. The building had been wired for light, but no connections had been made. So what to do now?

"Recreation and night prayers being finished," the diary says, "the Sisters proceeded to go to the

4. Ibid., 4.

dormitory." They borrowed a lantern from the watchman, and Sister Beatrix bravely led the procession. Somehow the light went out, and the group continued in total darkness.

Having arrived at the dormitory, they realized that they would need water! Two sisters volunteered to go in search, and with the help of the watchman, they triumphantly returned with a minimum requirement. Again, the diary communicates the spirit:

> One cake of soap was at the disposal of all. Surely this was community life, and well might this little band of missionaries liken themselves to "the early Christians," and exclaim, "Behold how we love each other" (or one another). An ideal community indeed, of but one heart and one soul. May this same spirit be always with the daughters of Our Lady of Victory.[5]

They were rewarded, the narrator tells us, by their finding a resting place. They could probably have slept standing up! But so passed the first night at OLV.

September 10 was spent in arranging dormitories and classrooms, a work they completed by evening. On the next day, Mr. Sharp brought his daughter and enrolled her as a boarder. Mrs. Sharp had been a boarder in Waco, and was eager for her

5. Ibid.

daughter to share the experience; but because the odor of fresh paint was overwhelming, the father took his child "to another of our houses." Fathers R. M. Nolan and V. Graffeo called on the sisters and were welcomed as their first guests.

September 11 found the sisters at St. Patrick's for Sunday Mass, and at St. Ignatius for breakfast.

> On Sunday afternoon, all the Sisters arrived at Our Lady of Victory and were ready to take charge of the work assigned them. They were Sister Margaret Mary, Sister Raphael, Sister Beatrix, Sister Marie Claire, Sister Mary Stanislaus, Sister Dorothy, Sister Lucian, Sister Joachim, Sister Mary Michael, Sister Victoria, Sister Mary Eugene, Sister Patricia, Sister Octavia, Sister Mary Loyola, and Sister Julia.[6]

Boarders began to arrive. Visitors were welcomed to tour the house. All went well until evening, when it was discovered that there was no light in the building. The electrician had locked the switchboard and put the key in his pocket. The watchman borrowed a lamp from a neighbor and placed it in the library, but as people continued to come, the sisters "found it very embarrassing to entertain a large group of people in total darkness." They called Mr. Sanguinet, who unscrewed the door

---

6. Ibid., 5.

to the switchboard and, to the relief of everyone, turned on the lights.

On September 12 the formal opening of school took place. Boarders who had been staying at St. Ignatius while awaiting their place at the new facility chattered excitedly; they were joined by new students who came from several towns of Texas and Oklahoma, so that, at the end of the day, thirty-one boarders and forty-one day pupils were registered. Since the boarders' refectory was not yet ready, an arrangement was made on the second floor, "at the cost of considerable inconvenience."

But classes had been promised for September 12, and classes there would be, in spite of sound of hammer and saw and the voices of workmen, and in spite of the overwhelming smell of fresh paint. There were laypersons involved in the project: teachers of art and music, of elocution and of physical education. Miss Dorchester, the art teacher, became ill during the night. The sisters called the watchman, who called Mr. Shaw, who called the ever-faithful Dr. Ray Saunders, who "responded promptly."

The diary entry for September 14 tells of another problem:

> Great trouble with the well. The tank is empty; consequently no water in the building. Water has to be carried by the Sisters from the first to the fifth floor to supply the

> wants of thirty-six boarders, also to be used in toilets. Mr. Hagan of Dallas suggests getting permission from Fireman Bidiker to have our tank filled from the fireman's hose. As this could not be done, a motor had to be placed in the engine house to force water into the house.[7]

On the fifteenth, "Mr. Orrick petitions the city council, in the name of the Sisters of St. Mary, to grade Shaw Street." The petition was granted, and action was prompt. On the sixteenth, "over fifty mules were employed all day" in that enterprise.

By October 7 the well was giving better satisfaction. On October 14 the elevator gave its first performance. (It broke down frequently, a habit in which it persevered throughout its natural life.) The altar arrived from Chicago on October 17, giving hope for the permanent chapel. The washing machine in the laundry was used for the first time on October 21. (How had they kept thirty-one boarders and the sisters clean for six weeks?) On October 24 Sister Mary Bernard supervised the unpacking of the altar. The first phone was installed on October 25. The first call was to St. Ignatius Academy.

On October 29 the furnace was lighted for the first time, and on the thirty-first a large number of workers were dismissed, since most of the work was finished. The Dallas Art Company delayed work

---

7. Ibid., 6.

in the chapel by not having the windows ready as promised.

There were always new challenges. Carmen Manly, who spoke only Spanish, arrived as a boarder. Sister Alphonsine Fulton undertook her education. In November, Father Carmelo Gagliardoni came from Dallas to hear her confession and instruct her for her first Holy Communion.

The "old boarders" arranged a celebration to welcome "new boarders" on November 1. It was surely a gala occasion, and refreshments were served afterwards.

A number of painters were dismissed, as was the night watchman, who had been employed by Miller and Son. OLV was on its own!

A strike in New York delayed delivery of chapel decorations. An agent arrived to take orders for vestments. On October 8, library cases were delivered and call bells were placed in the building; and on the tenth, the house phones were connected. The china kiln arrived on November 16, but it had been damaged in transit. Work in the chapel advanced, as electricians began installing fixtures.

On the feast of Saint Cecilia (November 22), the children presented an entertainment, and a "course dinner" was served at 6:00. The refectory was decorated in green, "the color of the Victorians." On the twenty-fourth, the boarders went to the opera with Miss Dorchester; and on that same day the first statue of the Blessed Virgin Mary arrived for OLV, gift of Mrs. J. P. Monahan, of New York. Other special events are noted: the arrival of basketball hoops; the placing of the first books in their cases.

Work began on chapel benches on December 1, crucifixes for the library were delivered soon afterward, and the Benziger representative arrived to receive an order for a sanctuary lamp, which was to be a gift from Mrs. Edward Devlin, of Ottawa, Canada, a memorial of her parents.

The sisters' refectory became ready on December 6, and December 11 was "parlor day" for the boarders. It is noted that there were many visitors; but there had been many visitors all along. Apparently people had a way of showing up and asking for a tour of the house, which was seen as a landmark.

During that week, the electricians finished mounting the chapel fixtures, and the boarders were invited to stop by the choir loft on their way to the dormitory. Awed by the beauty of the lighted chapel, they sang a hymn to our Lady.

A serious mishap occurred on December 17, when ladders supporting two electricians who were working on the arch of the sanctuary fell, injuring both men. Dr. Saunders treated one and drove the other to the "infirmary" in his own car. The altar was damaged in the accident.

Work continued, and on December 20 the remaining windows were placed in the chapel. On the twenty-third, the last workmen were dismissed, and on Christmas Eve, carpet was laid in the sanctuary, even while the sisters were decorating the altar with fern and white lilies. The sisters from St. Ignatius joined the local community in doing the singing for the Midnight Mass at OLV. Together they enjoyed Christmas dinner at St. Ignatius.

But there was always the debt. In the midst of their struggle to pay interest, not to mention principal, on the loan, they were delighted to learn that Hemphill was to be paved, but horrified to discover that both the paving and the curbing were to be at their expense. Everyone pitched in. The violin teacher gave a recital, as did the piano teacher; the elocution instructor offered a reading; all, perhaps, in hopes of having their salaries paid! A hand-painted vase was raffled, and a lace collar; a card game was sponsored; the high-school seniors presented a Japanese play. The few events that made a profit of at least $50.00 are reported as financially successful.

When the president of the paving company came to collect his fee, he reduced the cost somewhat, welcomed the cash available, and accepted a promissory note for the rest. He probably did not know that, besides earning money in various ways, the sisters had borrowed large amounts, some from the sisters in the North, some from the First National Bank.

All these happenings are described with little emotion, as is the fact that "Molly" has kicked and seriously hurt Mr. Hull. We assume that Molly is a cow. All the animals had names. We learn about "our beautiful Melissa," and when the Liberty Bell was on tour, and expected to pass through Fort Worth, the community named a new calf "Liberty Belle." But cattle rustling was not dead in Texas. "Our beautiful Jersey cow was stolen," as from the Baptist Seminary six cows were. Shortly afterwards, another cow was stolen, but "Patricia broke her rope and came home." Something had to be done. Mr. Russell came himself "to brand our animals."

Here, as from the earliest histories, laypeople were indispensable to the success of the project. Both men and women drove the sisters on errands or excursions in their own cars. There were donations that sustained: a cow was a treasured gift, and a cow with her calf, a special blessing. One benefactor gave an orchard; another, a pine tree; a third, a pig. There were the "tramps" who offered to "work for food"; one of these would milk the cows in exchange for meals and permission to sleep in the barn. He soon disappeared, along with the bedclothes he had been given. The Shaw Brothers' mule "fell dead in our yard while bringing us ice." Mr. Hull, a reliable employee who knew how everything worked, was taken to the hospital with a ruptured appendix. There was deep concern for him—and for the machinery in the laundry, which no one else could operate.

Wheat was planted west of the orchard, and the Baker Brothers put out other trees. There was rye too, and sorghum. We sense the quiet drama of the sisters' lives, as we read of the surprise visit of the parents of Sister Mechtilde Thorpe—their first in ten years. Shortly afterwards, when the father died, Mother Albertine wired Lockport for permission for Sister Mechtilde to attend the funeral.

In July of 1914, thirteen sisters made perpetual vows in the OLV chapel, and a few days later, Edith Gordon (whom we came to know as Sister Wilfred) left home to begin her novitiate in Lockport. In November of 1915 we are told that Sister Augusta McShea is not well, and three months later, that she has died. Sister Benedictine Bryson died in Denison. Excitement echoes in the news received on March 31, 1916: Pope Pius X has given our Rule official approval, making the Sisters of St. Mary a Pontifical Institute.

We were not, however, cloistered, nor was the house occupied only by sisters and students. Mrs. Reah's mother had a room on the fourth floor, and Mr. Tooms brought his mother to board. She too was given a room on the fourth floor. Her sons were attentive to her, bringing in a trained nurse when she became ill. She soon became a member of the larger family, as the diary refers to "dear Grandma Tooms." Her death was mourned by all.

We have the impression that OLV was a "finishing school," in the best tradition of the time. Not only did Sister Ferdinand Barnes and Sister St. Patrick come "to arrange the curriculum according to Washington," but lessons in music, art, and elocution were added. We read that, chaperoned by lay teachers, students occasionally went to operas; they were also taken to hear Mme. Tetrazzini sing. The latter accepted an invitation to come to OLV, and sang for the sisters. C. W. Griffith, an acclaimed reader of poems and plays, presented *Richard the Third*, and on another day read "Evangeline" in the morning and *Othello* in the evening. There was a reception for "bon ton ladies"; a "course meal" was served to the boarders. But there was no exclusiveness: "Home Economics Week" was observed; a "Texas missionary" spoke to the children about lives of saints; students attended lectures at the Chamber of Commerce; Miss Lemay came to give Spanish lessons to the sisters.

Daily Mass was celebrated, usually by the chaplain, a Vincentian priest, but a variety of priests are noted—some from "Dallas University," an occasional Jesuit, even the Vicar of St. Basil's College in Waco. Sister Bonaventure wrote from Ireland, reporting that she was enjoying her visit and hoping "to have many aspirants to take back to the U.S.A."

The first visitation of Mother Gonzague Maes to the American Province, in 1921, is marked by life-changing decisions. After visiting each of the houses in Canada, New York, and Texas, she writes:

> I am motherly and religiously proud to hear from so many good priests and religious, from so many distinguished seculars, from your venerated Bishops, much praise of our Institute and its work in America. . . . As some priests told me, you are, in a special manner, the necessary helps of the clergy in America. As a rule, the priests alone could not work efficaciously for the salvation of souls; many would escape their influence. But the Sisters draw the children, who unconsciously learn to like true religion in liking their teachers.[8]

Her long letter encourages the sisters to remain faithful to their "spirit of simplicity" and faithful to their vows, and to continue to be "true religious."

Surprisingly, there is no diary entry for April 8–29, nor do the March entries mention what must have been an earth-shaking event. We learn of it in another letter from Mother Gonzague:

> March 29, Easter Tuesday of 1921
>
> To All Our Dear Sisters
> In Belgium, America, and England.

---

8. Sisters of St. Mary of Namur, "Little Messenger of Mary," April–June 1921, 722.

My Very dear Sisters,

I gladly hasten to announce again great and good news to you.[9] Our eight Texas houses were this very day organized in a distinct province, which will always be very much attached to the Northern American Province and very grateful for all the generous sacrifices made in her behalf by Lockport since the early days of the first foundation nearly fifty years ago.

It is easy to understand that at a distance of nearly two thousand miles the Provincial Superior, endowed with the greatest abilities and devotedness, can hardly do justice to what depends on her, in the administration of eight houses with 130 Sisters, 7 Academies and Boarding Schools, 50 classes, and 2,500 pupils. This situation was fully grasped by our General Chapter; but the triennial visitation being at hand, the decision was put off for the time being.

This visitation, which has been greatly blessed by Almighty God, evidenced the pressing need of a Texas province. Rt. Rev. J. P. Lynch, Bishop of Dallas, fatherly interested in our community, graciously allowed the erection of a province of our Institute having its provincial house and its novitiate in his diocese. The General Council, the Ordinary

---

9. There had recently been an announcement that Canada had become a province.

of the motherhouse, and then the Holy See gave the necessary authorizations, and all things went on so speedily that the great news reached me on the eve of St. Joseph's feast, 18th of March, at the very moment when they were beginning in our European houses our great and solemn day of adoration. May the Lord be praised!

The Texan Provincial house will be the beautiful Academy of O.L.V., where nothing in the way of air and space and spiritual care will be wanting for our dear Novices.

The following nominations were made for three years:

> Provincial Superior, Mother John Berchmans, who will for the time being fulfill the charge of Mistress of Novices.

> First Councillor, Sister Julia, who will replace Sister John Berchmans as local superior in O.L.V.

I need not ask you to give your most cordial sympathy to our dear Texas province and to pray fervently for those to whom, for a time, its direction is confided. Fifty years ago, on Easter Tuesday, our venerated Mother Claire of Jesus was breathing her last. Some of her parting words were, "When I shall be in Heaven, how I shall pray for you . . . especially for the Superiors!" I trust that our dear Mother is actually accomplishing her promise, and more specially to-day. She prays for us and I ask her to bless us all, to obtain for all of us the great grace to become and remain her true and faithful children.

Most affectionately yours,

Mother Gonzague[10]

The news that Canada would be a province had hardly been surprising. The Canadian sisters lived under a different government from that of New York; they even spoke a different language. But Mother Gonzague had recognized that Texas too had different needs, no less deserving of respect. Travel distances from New York to Texas were even greater than those from New York to Canada. It was becoming increasingly clear that cultural differences existed. Texas girls were asking to be accepted into the Congregation. Their acceptance should be done locally, and their novitiate lived in the area in which they would serve. Texas needed both its own provincial government and its own novitiate.

Simple enough in itself, the announcement would have lasting consequences. There must have been rejoicing that novices would live nearer home; but what about the sisters who had come from New York or Canada to serve in Texas? Each was invited

---

10. SSMN archives, Fort Worth.

to choose the province to which she would now belong. We know of two Texans who chose to remain in New York, and there were many who had entered in New York who chose to continue their mission in Texas. Unity was not broken; representatives of each group would now meet in general chapters.

There would still be open channels of communication. *The Little Messenger*, and later *Echoes*, would report important events of each province, including news not only of the sisters but also of their parents. During World War II, when communication was difficult, sisters in the American provinces prayed each night for our sisters in Europe. Over the years, there have been exchanges of personnel. Sisters from each province continue to serve on the General Council, visiting each of the provinces. American, Canadian, and British sisters have joined the Belgians in serving in missions in Congo, Rwanda, Cameroon, Brazil, and Tanzania, and they are joined in mission by natives of each of those countries. The foundations in the Dominican Republic are served primarily by the Canadian Province, but have been joined by others in special projects.

Through a series of circumstances, the commitment to generalate and to other provinces was sometimes strained, would sometimes waver over the years. Faced with problematic decisions, communities of many religious congregations chose the simpler solution of becoming an entity separate from, though one in spirit with, the original foundation. For Sisters of St. Mary, the bond survived. Because it did, we were able to stand together through two world wars during which German-born sisters worked in our Texas province; Canadian, British, and American sisters worked with Belgian sisters not only in Texas but also in development of missions in Congo, Rwanda, Cameroon, and Tanzania; and African sisters went with sisters of northern provinces to open missions in Brazil. Because the bond held, non-African members stood beside our Rwandese sisters in the tragedy of the massacres there. In the twenty-first century, it is a source of pride that we are an international congregation, knowing and caring for one another in the ten countries we serve.

10

Personal Stories

Ours is a Congregation conceived in the midst of violence and poverty but born of the stronger power of love. Though the story you have read here comes from written documents, it is strongly influenced by oral tradition, because it is the lived example and the loved memories of the sisters that have been channels of God's grace for me, both in childhood and in my sixty-nine years of life in the Congregation.

Most of the stories come from sisters of our own Western Province, but I will first recall some I have from others of our worldwide community.

* * * * *

Sister Mary Augusta Escalier
Sister Mary Augusta Escalier was born in France during the time of religious suppression. As a young teen, she told her father that she wanted to be a

sister. He answered that he would listen no more to that desire until she reached her eighteenth birthday. When, on the designated day, she told him that the desire was still strong in her, he told her to talk to her pastor. The priest's reply was discouraging. "Our own sisters," he said, "are in northern Italy, waiting until they can return to France."

"But I don't want to wait!" she lamented. Then he told her of another possibility. He had a nephew who as a priest had established himself in Canada. There were sisters in his parish. Encouraged, but still with some hesitation, she once more approached her father.

Believing her vocation to be true, he gave an unexpected reply. "I've been thinking," he said, "that we might move to Canada so that your siblings could receive a Catholic education. We could go where our pastor's nephew is." The family farm was sold, and land was bought in Vankleek Hill, Ontario! The family would start over, still together.

When the transfer was accomplished and the family moved, the aspirant approached the Sisters of St. Mary in her new parish, only to learn that their novitiate was in New York, and the language there was English. With her parents' consent, she set out once more, like Abraham, to leave her family, her new country, even her language, to become Sister Mary Augusta, SSMN. Sister was advanced in years when, with remarkable simplicity, she told me her story. "Did you ever hesitate, or regret your decision?" I asked. And she answered, "How could I? God called me."

Sister Marie Julianne Farrington, long the provincial superior of the Eastern Province, and later general superior of the Congregation, confirmed my memory of the story, adding another detail. Before leaving France, Sister Mary Augusta's father, Hippolyte Escalier, had been among the men who, with infants in their arms, surrounded their parish church in defiance of an order to close it. Of such faith are vocations born. Truly, we stand on the shoulders of our ancestors.

* * *

Sister Agnes Connolly
Without the missionary spirit of the Irish, the history of the Sisters of St. Mary would have been very different, if indeed there would actually have been a history. My own experience bears witness to that. My first teachers at Sacred Heart Academy in Waco were Sister Gregory Connolly and Sister Colomba Ryan, and the superiors of the community successively were Sister Dominica Flood, Sister Benita Duggan, and Sister Benita's identical twin, Sister Francis Regis Duggan. All except Sister Dominica (who was Canadian) were from Ireland. Only much later did I learn something of the cost those pioneers paid for our evangelization. Let me

tell you a story of one of them, which turns out to be the story of several.

As a young girl, Hannah Connolly went from Killieraeby, Ireland, to Elmira, New York, to stay with some relatives. There she met the Sisters of St. Mary, and entered the community in Lockport, taking the name Sister Agnes. When the first mission in Texas was being started, Sister Agnes was assigned to Waco as one of the earliest missionaries.

Like all of our earliest Irish sisters, she accepted that her call meant that she would probably never see her family again. It happened, however, that after many years, she learned that her mother was gravely ill. The community of course joined her in prayer, but something more happened. Several sisters had been elected as delegates to the General Chapter (an international meeting held in Belgium). As they planned their trip, they realized that the boat would stop in Ireland. Could not Sister Agnes come that far with them? All were delighted with the plan.

As the ship was docking, Sister Agnes waved to her brother standing on the shore. Once landed, she hurried to greet him, only to receive the shocking news: "Our mother died while you were at sea."

It was Sister Agnes Collins, a niece of the earlier missionary (and also a Sister of St. Mary), who confirmed for me this story that I had read in the archives. "I often heard my mother say, 'Poor Sister

Agnes. The only time she came home, her mother died while she was on the high seas.'"

"Was the family embittered by this experience?" My question shocked my listener. "Oh, no," was the answer. "The family loved her very much—so much so that she was allowed to take her twin cousins back to the U.S. with her because their mother had died. They were only twelve years old, and went to school with the sisters in Texas before entering." (They became our much-beloved Sister Benita and Sister Francis Regis, mentioned above.) "Sister Gregory went at that time also, but she was eighteen and old enough to enter—as she wanted to do." Those three were always in the Texas province, the younger Sister Agnes recalled. (Her aunt, Sister Agnes, is buried in Waco.) And two other nieces, Sister Aiden Murphy and a sister of hers, became Sisters of St. Mary in the British province. One family, five missionaries.

We stand indeed on the shoulders of our ancestors!

* * *

Sister Martha Faecke
How did it ever happen? The small German settlement of Muenster, in North Texas, gave to the Congregation of the Sisters of St. Mary six of its most distinguished members, though no Sister of

St. Mary ever served there. The story offers another of the improbable events.

Elizabeth Catherine Faecke, a young Catholic woman from Denison, grew up at St. Xavier Academy. As valedictorian of her graduating class, she received and accepted a scholarship for postgraduate study with the Sisters of St. Mary in Lockport, New York. Returning to Texas with her teacher's certificate, she expected to be employed in a public school, but a problem arose. Catholicism was suspect in Texas; in the public schools, the Bible was included in the curriculum, but only the King James Version could be used, and Protestant theology was presupposed. The solution was found when Ms. Faecke received an appointment to the small Catholic town of Muenster! She served there and became known to the local community, but eventually left the assignment to enter the Sisters of St. Mary.

Shortly afterwards, a fervent Catholic family of Muenster sought a Catholic high school for their daughter. Would it be Ursuline Academy of Dallas? It had an excellent and long-established reputation. But there was a Catholic boarding academy in Fort Worth too, and Ms. Faecke was there. Ursula Endres would not feel so alone; someone else would know the people she knew, and the environment from which she came. And so the choice was for Our Lady of Victory Academy. Ursula eventually entered the community where, as Sister Agnes, she would develop a reputation as an outstanding religious, a master teacher, an elementary-school principal, and a supervisor of St. Mary schools in Texas and California. She would be followed into the community by her younger sister, Irma (religious as well as baptismal name), and various cousins, friends, and acquaintances; and all because Elizabeth Faecke had a problem getting a job!

* * *

Sister Mary Mathilda Laufkotter
This story is told by Judge Mary Sean O'Reilly
(Former Sister of St. Mary)

I met Sister Mathilda in 1964, when I was a sophomore at the Academy of Mary Immaculate in Wichita Falls, Texas. I think she was nearly eighty years old at that time. Sister Mathilda, with her heavy German accent, taught French to my sister Judy. My sister said Sister Mathilda was one of the best teachers she ever had.

Sister Mathilda spoke with me and Judy after school almost daily while we waited for our father to pick us up from school. She loved the fact that our mother taught in the Nursing School and that we had a large family. She loved world events and the News. Once she introduced us to her good friend Mother Elizabeth, who shared her love of Africa.

A few years later, when I was a canonical novice and working at OLV during the summer, I cared for Sister Mathilda, who was then living in the sisters' infirmary. One afternoon, we were just visiting and I asked her why she came to Texas, since she was born in Germany and our sisters were in Belgium. She told me that her father and older brother were doctors. Her father had a very fine reputation as a surgeon. He wanted her to have a good education, so he sent her to the Sisters of St. Mary in Namur.

Sister Mathilda's brother was required to fight in the First World War. He was killed during it. Mathilda's father was worried about her getting back to Germany, so he told her to stay in Belgium. She never saw her family again.

After finishing high school she joined the Community of the Sisters of St. Mary. Mathilda had a great desire to go to Africa when the sisters first went to Congo in the 1920s, and there was some discussion of that possibility. However, while she was a novice, Mathilda became very ill. She declined quickly, and lost her vision. The local doctor said it was mysterious but, due to the discharge coming out of her eyes, and her lack of comprehension, he thought it a probably fatal brain infection. Sister Mathilda told me that she remembered hearing the doctor speaking with the Novice Mistress, although Mathilda could not see or speak at that time. The doctor told the Novice

Mistress to tell the sisters that Mathilda would die in a day or two because her condition was worsening. He said that there was nothing that could be done, and that it was a shame since she was so young and intellectually gifted.

The doctor told the sisters that he had known Mathilda's father, who had been "a brilliant surgeon." He said there was one extreme measure he could take, with the sisters' consent, to attempt to save Mathilda's life. He said it was a procedure that had been discussed among surgeons but never tried, which required that he cut into her skull, locate the infection, and try to remove it. He warned the sisters that Mathilda would probably die during the procedure, but assured them she would not be in pain, since she was already unconscious. The sisters consented to the procedure.

The doctor later explained that once he had opened her skull and looked into her brain, he could see a massive infection, and that he simply began "spooning it out" in desperation. He then replaced the circle of skull bone, wrapped her head up, and waited for her to die. He told the sisters that it would be a miracle if she survived, but that if she did, she would be blind and probably mindless.

Several days later Mathilda awoke from her coma, and was able to speak. The sisters and doctor removed the bandages from her eyes, and she could see. She had a very long recovery, but her mind and memory were completely intact. The doctor could not believe the success of this first "brain" surgery and her full recovery.

Sister Mathilda asked to go to Africa once she recovered. However, the decision was made that she would not be allowed to be a missionary in Africa, due to the primitive medical conditions there and her "fragile" skull. She was heartbroken.

Some years later she was told that if she still wanted to be a missionary, she could go to the missions in Texas. She said God had granted the deepest wish in her heart—to serve as a missionary—so she went to Waco, Texas, and worked among the Hispanic people for almost forty years. She taught citizenship classes in the basement of the church. Thousands of Mexican families were granted U.S. citizenship as a result of her teaching. She told me that, more than once, the examining officials said that her students were always the best-prepared candidates.

I was told by other sisters that sometime in the 1960s the City of Waco named a portion of a city park "Mathilda Square" in her honor, but I have not been able to locate or confirm that information.

God works in such mysterious ways. Sister Mathilda was always so loving and patient with me and Judy. Her years and years of caring for others and self-abandonment gave her such a good heart. As an older and infirm sister, she was never demanding and always so gracious. I keep her death prayer card on my desk. I will always be so grateful and proud to have been her friend. God bless you, Sister Mathilda.

To appreciate adequately that miracle related by Judge O'Reilly, we need to know something of what came of it in Texas many years later. I quote here from Sister St. Patrick's doctoral dissertation, "A Brief History of the Foundation of the American Houses of the Sisters of St. Mary of Namur, Belgium," which is found in the archives of the Sisters of St. Mary in Fort Worth, Texas.

> In the early spring of 1921, at the suggestion of Rev. P. A. Heckman, then pastor of the Assumption Church, Sunday School classes were organized for the Mexicans in Waco. These classes, which later developed into a regular school, were from the very beginning under the direction of the Sisters of St. Mary of Namur.

Sufficient praise can never be given to Sister Mary Mathilda, who, appointed by her community to take charge of this work, arranged for the construction and development of the parish school of St. Francis, where she and others worked until the summer of 1946, when the Sisters of St. Mary of

Namur closed Sacred Heart Academy and withdrew from Waco.

Nor was this school, built on Sister Mathilda's passion for justice, the only work of its kind committed to her community. Sister St. Patrick reports:

> It was in 1926 that Bishop Lynch, of Dallas, asked the Sisters of St. Mary to take charge of San José Mission School for Mexicans in North Fort Worth. The Sisters consented, and worked zealously there until 1958, when the San José parish was incorporated with All Saints Parish. . . . The children of San José now attend All Saints' parochial school.

Once more, in 1927,

> . . . the Bishop requested the Sisters of St. Mary to organize and care for the Mexican Mission School of Our Lady of Guadalupe in Wichita Falls.

That parish has since built its own school.

This heritage, which we claim as our own (though seldom without mentioning Sister Mathilda), is now expressed not only in schools, but also in parish work with the Spanish-speaking community. We ask Sister Mathilda's support as we seek ways to serve new immigrants.

* * * * *

The sisters named above were chosen not because of their national origin, but simply because of the uniqueness of each of their stories. It is worth noting, however, that each life began in a different country: Sister Mary Augusta was from France, Sister Agnes from Ireland, and Sister Mathilda from Germany, while Sister Martha's homeland was the United States. Responding together to the needs of the time, each generation answers the same call to announce the Good News of God's Kingdom.

Time Chart

THIS CHART suggests the atmosphere in which the early foundations were made, and the cultural changes that affected their development.

1836	Texas independence declared (No resident priests in Texas)
1844	Telegraph comes into use
1845	Texas joins the Union
1847	Bishop Odin named first Bishop of Galveston
1860s	Civil War divides the nation
1861	Texas secedes from Union
1870	Texas readmitted to Union
1871	Compulsory-education law passed; weak enforcement
1872	Sisters of St. Mary arrive in Denison, on Dec. 24; MKT Railroad connects North and South

1873	September: Sisters arrive in Waco	
	First Catholic church of Texas built in Denison	
1874	Sisters arrive in Corsicana	
1876	Sisters arrive in Denison	
1877	Sisters arrive in Sherman	
	End of post-Civil War reconstruction	
1885	Sisters settle in St. Ignatius Academy, Fort Worth	
1889	Railroad reaches Wichita Falls	
1902	Academy of Our Lady of Good Counsel (later replaced by Bishop Dunne High School), Dallas	
1904	Academy of Our Lady of the Rosary, Ennis	
1905	Academy of Mary Immaculate (later replaced by Queen of Peace School), Wichita Falls	
1910	Our Lady of Victory Academy (later replaced by Nolan High School), Fort Worth	
1912	St. Edward's Academy, Dallas	
1921	Western Province established	
Note:	As public transportation and private cars became available, the need for boarding schools diminished. The movement was towards parochial schools and catechetical programs.	

1925	St. Francis Mission School, Waco
1926	St. Anne Parochial School, Porterville (California)
	San José Mission School, Fort Worth
1927	Our Lady of Guadalupe Mission School, Wichita Falls
1928	St. Mary Parochial School, Fort Worth
1929	Catechetical centers in parishes (in Fort Worth: Immaculate Heart, San Mateo, and Our Lady of Guadalupe)
1930	Sacred Heart Parochial School, Hollister (California)
1936	St. Cecilia Parochial School, Dallas
1937	St. Anne Parochial School, Beaumont
	Resurrection Parochial School, Houston
1940	St. James Parochial School, Dallas
1942	St. Alice Parochial School, Fort Worth
1946	Shrine of the True Cross Parochial School, Dickenson
1954	St. Maria Goretti Parochial School, Arlington
	St. Andrew Parochial School, Fort Worth
1955	Queen of Peace Parochial School, Wichita Falls
1956	University of Dallas, Irving

1960 St. Mary Novitiate, Irving
1961 Nolan High School, Fort Worth
      Bishop Dunne High School, Dallas
      John XXIII School, Dallas
Note: Since about 1960, ministry has no longer been confined to schools and catechetical programs. Communities or individuals have served in various ways at such places as St. Maria Convent (on Grant Street in Fort Worth), St. Thomas University (Houston), St. John the Apostle (Fort Worth), and West Texas Ministries.

A mission established in Zihuatanejo, Mexico, closed after three years for lack of available personnel, but sisters of the Western Province have served in missions in Africa, Brazil and the Dominican Republic.

Over the years, as well-prepared lay administrators and teachers became available, the schools were turned over to them, and more sisters became engaged in diocesan and parish ministries. The trend continues into the twenty-first century.

Works Consulted

Published Works

Corcoran, Sister Mary Louise, SSMN. *Seal of Simplicity: The Life of Mother Emilie, First Superior in America of the Sisters of St. Mary of Namur*. Westminster, MD: Newman Press, 1958.

Dederichs, Sister Joseph A., and Sister Rose Mary Cousins. *Catholic Schools: Dawn of Education in Texas*. Beaumont: Beaumont Printing and Lithographing, 1986.

Hoover, William R. *St. Patrick's: The First 100 Years*. Fort Worth: St. Patrick Cathedral, 1988.

Knight, Oliver. *Fort Worth: Outpost on the Trinity*. Fort Worth: Texas Christian University Press, 1990.

Langford, Sister Mary Diane, CDP. *The Tattered Heart: A Historical Fiction Biography of Mother St. Andrew Feltin, CDP*. New York: Universe, Inc., 2007.

Maguire, Jack. *Katy's Baby: The Story of Denison, Texas*. Austin: Nortex Press, 1991.

Moore, James Talmadge. *Through Fire and Flood: The Catholic Church in Frontier Texas, 1836–1900*. College Station: Texas A&M University Press, 1992.

Selcer, Richard F. *Hell's Half Acre: The Life and Legend of a Red-Light District*. Chisholm Trail Series 9. Fort Worth: Texas Christian University Press, 1991.

Turley, Sister Mary Immaculata, SHG. *Mother Margaret Mary Healy-Murphy: A Biography*. San Antonio: Naylor Co., 1969.

Van Der Essen, Léon, *A Short History of Belgium*. Chicago: University of Chicago Press, 1920.

Unpublished Materials

A Sister of St. Mary of Namur. "Life of Mother Emilie of St. Cecilia." Archives, Our Lady of Victory Center, Fort Worth.

A Sister of St. Mary of Namur. "Mère Delphine: Sa vie et l'histoire de l'Institute sous son Generalat." Archives, Our Lady of Victory Center, Fort Worth.

A Sister of St. Mary of Namur. "Nicholas Joseph Minsart: Founder of the Sisters of St. Mary of Namur." Archives, Our Lady of Victory Center, Fort Worth.

Academy of Mary Immaculate. "Book of Personnel, 1905–1998." Archives, Notre Dame Catholic School, Wichita Falls, TX.

Academy of Mary Immaculate. "Minutes of Meetings of the Board of Trustees: December 1906–April 1958. Archives, Notre Dame Catholic School, Wichita Falls, TX.

Academy of Mary Immaculate. "Triennial Visitation Books, 1921–1998." Archives, Notre Dame Catholic School, Wichita Falls, TX. (Of special interest is File 9 of the Book for 1921–1928: "Sisters of St. Mary in Texas, Important Letters.")

Kelly, Sister Barbara, SSMN. "Academy of Mary Immaculate: The School That Faith Built." Archives, Our Lady of Victory Center, Fort Worth.

Kemen, Mother Emilie. "Letter to Bishop Dubuis: January 24, 1874." Catholic Archives of Texas, Austin, Texas.

Mars, Sister Adelaide, SSMN. "A History Sketch of Our Lady of Good Counsel Academy, 1902–1961." Archives, Our Lady of Victory Center, Fort Worth.

McConville, Sister St. Patrick, SSMN. "A Brief History of the Foundation of the American Houses of the Sisters of St. Mary of Namur, Belgium." Archives, Our Lady of Victory Center, Fort Worth.

Mooney, Sister Constance, SSMN. "Book of Parishes, Schools, and Priests." Archives, Our Lady of Victory Center, Fort Worth.

Sisters of St. Mary of Namur. "Little Messenger of Mary," 1910–1925. Archives, Our Lady of Victory Center, Fort Worth.

www.ingramcontent.com/pod-product-compliance
Lightning Source LLC
Chambersburg PA
CBHW071447150426
43191CB00008B/1268